THE CHURCH ON THE HILL

The First Hundred Years of
All Saints Episcopal Church
Great Neck, New York
1886-1986

BY MARIE B. HECHT
Preface by the Reverend Gary E. Maier

C.T.F. print inc., New York, New York

*To the Founding Fathers of All Saints Church
and
To Rudolph Kopf – Munificent Benefactor*

Contents

PREFACE

Many people have offered substantial portions of their lives to the worship and work of All Saints Church. We see in this volume a history of commitment to Jesus Christ, His Church, the Great Neck community and beyond. This Church history, three years in preparation, is the culmination of one parishioner's offering.

Marie B. Hecht became a member of All Saints Church under unusual circumstances. While recuperating after a tragic auto accident which almost claimed her life, she had a vision. Our Lord appeared to her. In response, Marie asked if I would come to see her for prayer and spiritual guidance. As she slowly recovered from her many injuries, she made a commitment to Jesus Christ and to His Church. Today, Marie serves as the first woman Warden of this parish.

Marie Hecht is a noted author and historian. She has written many books. Her most recent major works, published by Macmillan, are *Beyond the Presidency* and *Odd Destiny: The Life of Alexander Hamilton.* Her writing has received national acclaim.

As we come to the close of the 100th anniversary year, we are grateful for the work of the clergy and laity of All Saints parish. We are particularly grateful to our present Bishop, The Rt. Rev. Robert Campbell Witcher, an historian in his own right, for his untiring support and strength.

I hope that reading these pages you will relive the past of All Saints and know that we have been guided by God's Love. We also know that the future of this parish will be strengthened by the power of Jesus Christ through His Holy Spirit.

I congratulate Marie Hecht for the success of her efforts and I ask that God's Spirit will be with you all as you read the book.

Faithfully yours in Christ,

The Rev. Gary E. Maier
Rector of All Saints Church
August, 1987

All Saints Church, 1987

1

THE FOUNDING: The Ministry of Louis De Cormis

At the time of the founding of All Saints Church, Great Neck was a wealthy community of estates, farms and a tiny village located near the northern end of the Great Neck peninsula. There was no Episcopal Church on the Neck so that Great Neck Episcopalians had to travel a considerable distance by horse and buggy to Christ Church, Manhasset.

An alternative was to attend the Union Free Chapel, located near the present day Village Green, which Richard Allen had given as a place of worship for any Christian denomination. Here Reverend Homan, the Rector of Christ Church, Manhasset conducted semi-monthly evening services and supervised an afternoon Sunday School for the children. After his death in 1882, the new Christ Church Rector, Charles L. Newbold, continued the work. The need for an Episcopal Church in the area was keenly felt.

In the early 1850's, Thomas Messenger arrived in the United States from the Isle of Wight with a cargo of Jersey cows to start a farm. He bought an estate in Great Neck running between Main Street and East Shore Road to the water. It prospered and, when he died, Messenger left a bequest of $7500 toward the erection of a Great Neck Church on the condition that the residents of the Neck raised an additional $2500. The bequest was not directed to anyone in particular. However, since Mr. Messenger had been a pew holder at Christ Church, Manhasset at the time of his death, the Vestry of Christ Church appointed a committee to invite residents of Great Neck to act on the legacy. The Great Neck gentlemen declined to cooperate with the Christ Church Vestry. Instead, they started to take action on their own.

On the evening of June 30, 1886, a group of Great Neck citizens met in the district schoolhouse to initiate proceedings on Messenger's bequest. They decided to circulate a subscription paper in order to raise the necessary sum of $2500. Enthusiasm for the project was enhanced further when the announcement was made that Thomas Messenger's two daughters, Miss M. Girard Messenger and Mrs. Charles C. Gignoux, had offered to contribute a beautiful site on the western reaches of their estate to be used for the church, a rectory, a parish house and a cemetery.

The Hon. John A. King called a second meeting in the district schoolhouse in September at which Joseph L. Hewlett presided. With great joy, Mr. King informed the gathering that the demands of the Messenger bequest had been more than met—$3400 had been subscribed already. Much encouraged, the gathering appointed a three-man committee, composed of King, Hewlett and Edward Morgan, and directed it to claim the $7500 from Thomas Messenger's executors for "the erection of a church building upon Great Neck for the celebration of divine worship according to the rites, discipline and canons of the Protestant Episcopal Church in the Diocese of Long Island." The committee was instructed further to accept with gratitude the offer of land from Miss Messenger and Mrs. Gignoux.

In a short time, Mr. King was able to report that the executors of the Messenger estate had agreed to turn over the legacy as soon as the church was incorporated. A committee of five, which was appointed to do this, petitioned the Rector, Wardens and Vestrymen of Christ Church, Manhasset "to bless the further work of the people of Great Neck by giving consent that this portion of Christ Church, Manhasset be conceded to the new church." A 1903 historical sketch of Christ Church, Manhasset recorded that "much dread" was felt by many that the establishment of the Great Neck church would cause the depletion of Christ Church because a large amount of parish support came from residents of Great Neck who would no longer be contributors. Nevertheless the Christ Church Vestry granted the petition and, as it happened, neither church suffered financially. Mr. Newbold, the Christ Church Rector, expressed his approval of the fine work of the committee and wished the new parish God-speed.

To satisfy the rules for the certificate of incorporation, at two morning services previous to the October 18, 1886 incorporation meeting, George

The Hon. John A. King, a founder of All Saints Church

Hewlett read publicly the notice of the establishment of a Protestant Episcopal church in Great Neck, New York. On that date, there being no rector, George Hewlett called the meeting to order. Two wardens were elected, John Alsop King and George Hewlett, and it was decided to have five vestrymen: Charles C. Gignoux, John Birbeck, Edmund C. Stanton, Edward Morgan and John Brown. The Church was to be known as All Saints Church, Great Neck, New York.

The first services of the newly incorporated parish, which were held in the Great Neck Mission Free Church, were conducted by George Webster Peck, a layman and vestryman of St. George's Church, Flushing. The first communion service, held in the same place, was celebrated by Dr. John C. Smith, Rector of St. George's and the first sermon, preached by Dr. Carpenter, was declared by the vestry to be "very appropriate and soul stirring."

The building of the church on top of Regan's Hill was the major concern of the new vestry. All agreed that it should be a handsome, substantial edifice worthy of its setting and its congregation and, of course, a fitting House of God. Renwick, Aspinwall & Russell, the distinguished architects of St. Patrick's Cathedral in New York City were engaged to submit plans. The result was a solid but charming grey stone structure, modeled on the English rural church, aptly referred to by Bishop Littlejohn, Long Island's first Bishop, as "a bit of Old England."

James L'Hommedieu, who had a large coal and lumber yard and belt-driven mill on East Shore Road where the oil tanks now stand and had just finished extensive building in Garden City for M.A.T. Stewart, was chosen to be the builder.

All Saints Church, early 1900's before the widening of Middle Neck Road

The greystone used for construction was found on the property and in nearby fields. Robert Ellard, who as a small boy watched the construction of All Saints, described the process of preparing and mounting the stones. The rocks were blasted and broken to a size that could be handled and then dragged on stoneboats by teams of horses to the circle section. There a canvass covered shelter housed a number of Scottish stonedressers who shaped and dressed the stones. Stone drillers, stationed all around the working area, drilled holes in the rocks into which the blasting charges were placed ready for the late day blasting. The drillers were paid by the inch according to the size of the holes drilled. Many of the masons were local men.

When the walls of the building rose too high above the ground for a man to reach, platforms were built. The stones were then wheeled up the inclines in wheelbarrows, a feat that required great strength especially for the stones that had to be taken up to the tower.

The first Tiffany window installed in the church

The interior of the church was faced with brick in two colors, cream and terracotta. The roof was of yellow pine and the furniture of ash and oak. The windows were light colored diamond glass except for the first stained glass window. This was an effective design made by the Tiffany Glass Company, an early and subtly colored example of their craftsmanship. It was given in memory of their small daughter by Mr. and Mrs. Edmund C. Stanton of New York.

Donations of furniture and stone, glass, brass, wood and silver enhanced the beauty of the interior and revealed the generosity and exquisite taste of the donors. A stone memorial font, contributed by Mr. and Mrs. Charles C. Gignoux, carved under the direction of Moffitt, well known for the imposing entrance to Greenwood cemetery, Brooklyn, stood in the baptistry near the entrance to the church. An eagle lectern, one of Lamb's largest and most imposing, was an offering from Mrs. William Smith of Great Neck. Mrs. Edward Winslow of New York gave a solid, magnificently carved oak bishop's chair. The Queen Anne design communion service in solid silver from the Gorham Company was given by Mrs. Chauncey Hamilton and Miss Clara Messenger, nieces of Thomas Messenger. The hymn tablets in heavy oak were given by Mrs. James Gore King of New York. The chancel furniture was designed for the church.

While the church was being built and furnished, the congregation met at the Union Chapel. In May, 1887, All Saints Church applied for membership and was admitted into union with the churches of the diocese of Long Island, agreeing to observe all the canons, rules, orders and regulations of the convention.

The following month, the Vestry elected a committee composed of Messrs. King, Gignoux and Morgan to call a clergyman. At this time, the Vestry also laid out the grounds for a cemetery and petitioned the Board of Supervisors of Queens County for the power to use a certain portion of the church land for a cemetery. In addition, at that same meeting, authorization was given to purchase such necessary church furnishings as cushions, hassocks, furniture for the church and a small organ. And, most important of all, November 1, 1887 was set aside for the consecration of the church and the Bishop was to be invited to perform the ceremony.

The search committee, with the consent of the rest of the vestry, decided to call the Reverend Louis De Cormis to take charge of the parish beginning on October 15th. Mr. De Cormis, D.D., LLD., had been the rector of St. Stephen's, Lynn, Massachusetts for ten years and was currently the assistant minister at St. Ann's Church, Brooklyn. He was a native of Norfolk, Virginia, where his paternal ancestors had lived for generations, a graduate of Kenyon College, Ohio and, in 1873, from the Episcopal Theological School in Cambridge, Massachusetts.

We, the Rector, Churchwardens *and* Vestrymen
of All Saints Church Great Neck, Long Island

and State of New York having, by the good Providence
of Almighty God, erected in the said place a house of
public worship, do hereby appropriate and devote the same to the worship
and service of Almighty God, the Father, the Son, and the Holy Ghost,
according to the provisions of the Protestant Episcopal Church in the
United States of America, in its Ministry, Doctrines, Liturgy, Rites,
and Usages, and by a Congregation in communion with said Church, and
in union with the Convention thereof in the Diocese of Long Island

And we do also hereby request the Right Reverend Abram
Newkirk Littlejohn D.D. LLD Bishop of the said Diocese, to take
the said building under his spiritual jurisdiction as Bishop aforesaid, and that
of his successors in Office, and to consecrate the same by the name of
All Saints Church.
and thereby separate it from all unhallowed, worldly and common uses,
and solemnly dedicate it to the holy purposes above mentioned.

And we do moreover hereby relinquish all claim to any right of
disposing of the said building, or allowing of the use of it in any way
inconsistent with the terms and true meaning of this Instrument of
Donation, and with the consecration hereby requested of the
Bishop of this Diocese.

In Testimony whereof, We, the said Rector, Churchwardens
and Vestrymen, have caused this Instrument of Donation to have
attached to it the seal of our Corporation, and the signatures of
the Presiding Officer and Clerk of a meeting duly convened on this
twenty first day of October in the year of our
Lord one thousand eight hundred and eighty seven.

Louis DeCormis Rector

John A. King
George Hewlett
Edward Morgan
Charles _____
_____ _____
John C. Brown
Nehemiah Hayden

} Wardens

} Vestrymen

The Instrument of Donation of All Saints Church

The long awaited Festival of All Saints, 1887 fell on a Tuesday. It was an overcast day but the weather did not dim the enthusiasm of the congregation that filled the church to overflowing. The Bishop of Long Island, assisted by a large number of the clergy, consecrated All Saints Church. Mrs. Gignoux played the organ and the choir, all church members, sat in the front pews.

The Reverend J. Carpenter Smith, D.D. of Flushing, Long Island preached the sermon. He spoke of mankind's need for a "sacred place" based on instinct, law and tradition. The customs of the Jews and then the Christians give sanction for consecrating such a place, he said. And, he added, this idea fits in with the needs and usages of the present day.

Bishop Littlejohn then delivered a eulogy on the late Thomas Messenger, founding father of the new church. He mentioned Messenger's consecrated generosity to other churches—St. Ann's, Brooklyn, St. Paul's, Paris, and the chimes that he had given to the American Church in Rome. The administration of Holy Communion followed the eulogy.

After the service, the congregation went to the magnificent Gignoux home for a superb luncheon. A little girl who attended the elegant affair remembered many years later the variety of dishes that were served and especially the desserts, edifices made of nougat and candied fruit decorated with confections of spun sugar.

Two years after the church was completed, Rev. De Cormis persuaded Mr. King that a rectory was a necessary part of parish equipment. The new rectory was built according to the plans of Renwick, Aspinwall & Russell of New York by James L'Hommedieu. The spacious house was constructed of granite to the second story and then of slate on the second and third stories. The materials were chosen to be in harmony with the stone church and to add to its dignity and impressiveness. All modern conveniences such as gas, water, and electric bells were included and the members of the parish furnished the rectory handsomely. Bishop Littlejohn remarked that so many rectories that he had seen were "Queen Anne in front but Mary Anne behind." The All Saints rectory, however, was "Queen Anne on all sides." The beautiful plantings in the rectory garden were contributed by the Gignoux estate and the enclosure by George Hewlett. Upon its completion, the De Cormises moved in to become the All Saints Church rectory's first tenants.

An analysis of the cost of the church property up to this time (October, 1889) was issued to the parishioners. The cost of the church building and furnishings including an estimate of the memorials and gifts came to $31,731.75 and the cost of the rectory to $13,500.00. The Vestry explained that the seemingly large expenses were justified "by the desire to have the church property placed in such a substantial condition as will require very few repairs for many years to come, and as will prove a source of pleasure and pride not only to the members of the Parish, but to the entire community of Great Neck."

The church was entirely paid for but there was a deficit of $4,156.39 owed on the rectory. To eradicate the debt, the Vestry arranged that a special collection be taken up on Sunday, November 3, 1889. Generous contributions quickly settled the debt.

On that same Sunday, a handsome double stained glass window was unveiled in memory of Mrs. Sheldon Goodwin. The window, which was six months in the making at the famous works of Heaton, Butler & Bayne of England, was installed under the supervision of the Gorham Manufacturing Company of New York. St. John the Baptist and St. John the Evangelist were the subjects of the new window, an unusual pairing. But, a contemporary newspaper reported, "suggestive and impressive and the poses and coloring are models of conception and execution."

The Churchyard: A modest beginning (early 1900's)

In November, 1889, the Bishop of Long Island came to All Saints Church for confirmation and for the consecration of the new cemetery. In a dramatic sermon, the Bishop spoke of the stability of certain aspects of religion such as Baptism, Confirmation and Holy Communion as evidenced by their survival through so many centuries. The large congregation was deeply moved by his words. After this, Bishop Littlejohn led the flock to the rear of the Church to consecrate the cemetery, "a lovely tract of land stretching far along the north side of the church including several acres." The area, beautifully laid out by Vaux and Co., professional landscape gardeners, had winding paths lined with carefully selected shrubbery making a lovely, restful spot. After the open air service, the procession, again led by Bishop Littlejohn, moved to the rectory for a service of benediction. The crowd of worshippers filled the hall, parlors and piazza.

Angels with musical instruments (Tiffany Window - 1891)

Another new memorial window, was installed in All Saints Church on August 23, 1891, the gift of Harris C. Childs of the firm of Root & Childs, New York, in memory of his wife and daughter. The window is divided into four panels. The center sections contain cartoons of Perugino angels clothed in flowing drapery, their voices raised in sacred song accompanied by musical instruments held in their hands. The two end panels each have a legend from the Te Deum set in the midst of variegated opalescent glass which shades off into the central panels. The window, which commemorates Mrs. Childs' unusual musical gifts given generously in the service of the church, is an outstanding specimen of the Tiffany Glass Company's use of opalescent glass of rich and varied colors.

Among the most important organizations started at All Saints Church in its early years was the Girls Industrial School founded in 1889. Its annual session began the first Saturday in Advent and closed the last Saturday in Lent. The personnel of the school consisted of about fifty students and teachers. Beginning students entered the "patchwork class" and, as they improved, progressed to plain sewing, the buttonhole class and, finally, the most difficult, to the darning class. Mrs. De Cormis, who founded the school, added an embroidery class in 1895 as an incentive to better work and to retain the older students whom, she hoped, she could persuade to stay on as teachers. Adults were admitted if they were proficient in plain sewing.

The school met every Saturday morning from 10-11:20 and the cost of the materials was met by contributions. The purpose of the program, said Mrs. De Cormis, was to increase neatness in dress, personal cleanliness, helpfulness at home and provide an opportunity for self support. Mrs. De Cormis added that "Cleanliness, self-reliance and good morals make good preparation for religion."

At the annual exhibition of the Sewing School in April 1895, its sixth year, a ceremony was held with the eight teachers and sixty-five students present. Two hundred and twenty three pieces had been completed by the students at the school that year. Twenty-eight students received prizes for punctuality and one a silver thimble for doing the best work in the buttonhole class. Mr. and Mrs. Gignoux had presented silver thimbles at each year's closing ceremony and, though absent in Germany during the 1895 exhibition, the Gignouxs did not to forget to provide their annual treat of ice cream for all at the closing exercises.

Another active and productive society founded at about the same time, was the Pastoral Aid and Missionary Society. It held two sessions each year, one at the Advent season and one at the Lenten season. The meetings were held on Tuesday mornings from 10-12 at the members' residences. Much of the sewing was done at the meetings but if the quota decided upon was not met, garments were given to needy persons to finish for which they were paid.

The meetings of the Society, to which all of the women of the parish were invited, were opened with a prayer and closed with the saying of the doxology. However, the gatherings were informal and social, always including light refreshments. Recipients of the garments made by the Society were chosen by the group. For example, the work of the Advent series, 1893, was donated to St. Phoebe's Mission, Brooklyn.

On June 9, 1892, a two ton bell, cast at the Shane Foundry, Baltimore in the same mould as the Cathedral Chimes at Garden City, was placed in the All Saints Church tower. An impressive Benediction Service was conducted by Rev. De Cormis. At the close of morning services, the Rector left the chancel, passed down the aisle, the congregation standing, and took his place to the east of the bell. The Rector called on God to "bless, hallow and sanctify" this bell, praying that it may, "through many generations, call together the people to praise and worship."

The first stroke on the bell, which had inscribed the legend, "All Saints Church, N.Y., 1892, Qui Audit, Dicat Veni," was made by J.L. Hewlett, the largest contributor to it and the oldest citizen in Great Neck. The bell was the forefather of the beautiful chimes and clock installed later.

In 1894, Bishop Littlejohn chose All Saints Churchyard for the site of his burial. He wrote to the Vestry that he had looked over every parish cemetery in the Diocese as the possible final resting place for himself and his family when, at last, "I thought of the ground adjoining All Saints, therefore that spot will be constantly in my mind's eye," and "will have an interest attaching to none other upon earth." The first Bishop of Long Island thanked the Rector and Vestry of All Saints Church and assured them of "my affection and confidence in them as the trustees and guardians of my mortal remains when the dear Lord shall see fit to call me hence."

At his death, Bishop Littlejohn left a bequest of $500 to the Corporation for the care of the "God's Acre." He had often said to the Rector that so large and so fine a property should have an endowment at least sufficiently large to provide against the misfortunes that time and chance are so apt to bring.

Another elegant Tiffany Glass window was placed in All Saints Church in May, 1895. In construction for a year, it was given to the glory of God in memory of the late Harry Messenger and his wife Rose by their five children: Mrs. Samuel T. Skidmore, Mrs. R.C. Hamilton, Mrs. L. Soutter Lowry and the Messrs. Fred and Albert Messenger of New York.

Competent observers commented that the new window had never been surpassed in design, mechanical features and artistic treatment by any other work sent out by the famous company. The subject of the large window is four of the Beatitudes from Jesus' Sermon on the Mount (Matt. 5:3-10) — those blessing the Poor, the Meek, the Pure and the Peacemakers—depicted amidst warm blue oriental skies, hillsides and varied exquisite faces and draperies. A contemporary journalist wrote that the window was indeed a most attractive and instructive feature "in this much admired church." The unveiling of the window took place on Ascension Day.

The All Saints Church Sunday School opened on Whitsunday, June 2, 1895. More persons than could be used at the time offered to teach in the school. The aim of the school, the Rector said, will be to have religious instruction that is "definite, thorough and systematic." He explained that the same system of grading, promotion and prizes that worked so well in the Sewing School would be used. And, in addition to the annual Picnic and Christmas Tree, other attractive exercises were planned for the students. Its ultimate purpose, Rev. De Cormis said, was to "so closely connect the Sunday School with the Church that the children will easily and naturally pass on to church membership." In less than two months after the school opened, 75 students were enrolled.

With some surprise and disappointment, the Vestry accepted the resignation of Mr. De Cormis to take effect in the fall of 1895.

The reasons for his decision were not made public. *The Review*, a publication to which Mr. De Cormis contributed regularly, wrote that "at the request of the Rector and out of regard for him we refrain from further comment or statement in regard to the resignation." According to the same source, "all his congregation are feeling very badly about it (the resignation) and will petition the Vestry to reconsider their decision . . . and . . . may also petition the rector to withdraw his resignation and stay with them." No further information on why the Rector chose to leave has been discovered.

The fact remains that Mr. De Cormis left All Saints Church after nine years of service. His record of achievement was admirable. He confirmed 48, married 25, buried 49 and baptized 122 persons. Under his leadership, the Church was finished, paid for and consecrated. The cemetery was consecrated and the bell was installed as well as many memorial windows. Contributions reached nearly $70,000 and several funds which had been started were growing steadily. Highly successful parochial agencies had been established: a Pastoral Aid Society, a large Sewing School and a Sunday School. Warden John A. King wrote of Mr. De Cormis that "he was at all times able by preaching and conversation to give full evidence of careful training, intellectual capacity" and "of being a diligent seeker after knowledge and truth."

The Rev. Kirkland Huske, 2nd Rector of All Saints

2

COMING OF AGE: The Ministry of Kirkland Huske

Kirkland Huske was chosen to be the second rector of All Saints. Finding the parish in a somewhat chaotic condition, he immediately started to systematize the work and to strengthen those areas that he deemed to be weak. He particularly wanted to increase the congregation's interest in diocesan affairs and in missionary activities. And also among his first priorities were the building of a Parish House and the strengthening of the Sunday School. Mr. N.S. Rulison described Mr. Huske, shortly after he took over his duties at All Saints, as a gentleman born and bred with an attractive personality and charming manners. He is "a good reader, preacher, pastor and worker and has made a deep impression on his parish."

Less than a month after he came to Great Neck, Mr. Huske started the Altar Guild and appointed Mrs. George W. Skidmore to serve as its first president. He also introduced a regular 8 P.M. Sunday evening service at which each week a prominent speaker was invited to address the congregation.

At the ninth anniversary of the consecration of All Saints and the first anniversary of the dedication of the eleven chancel windows, made in London by Heaton, Butler & Baine and given in memory of Thomas and Anne Messenger, the Rector preached a sermon called "The Kingdom." Its purpose was to explain the meaning of the windows. "Look upon

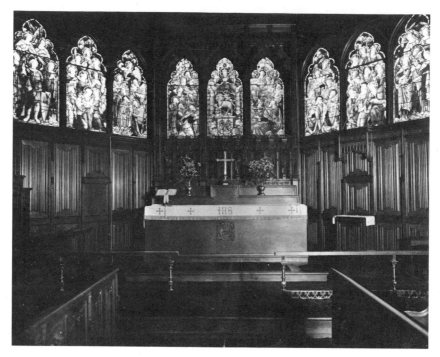

All Saints Church Sanctuary and Chancel Windows

these chancel windows. What do we see?" asked Rev. Huske. "The God-man upon the throne; in His Hand the Book of Life sealed with seven seals which none may open save the Lion of the tribe of Judah." A rainbow encircles the throne symbolizing God's covenant with Noah after the great flood.

In front of the throne are the four beasts; the lion, the calf, the beast with the face of a man and the flying eagle. These represent the four beings that hold primacy in the world. Among created beings, man; among birds, the eagle; among cattle, the ox; and among wild animals, the lion.

We see also torches of fire before the throne. These are not to remind us of the fire of judgment but of the baptism of the Holy Spirit which is a baptism of fire. The flaming presence purges the spirit from sin and consumes evil whether in men's minds, men's lives or the world.

In the midst of the throne and the four living beings stands the lamb with seven horns, which denote completeness and strength. Signs of suffering are visible on the lamb for He represents Him, "who through life died and is alive forevermore." In the next four windows, we see, on either side of the throne, twenty-four elders with crowns on their heads and harps in their hands. These fall down before Him saying, "Thou art worthy to receive honor and power and glory." They are kings and priests and there are twenty-four of them because they represent the two Testaments—the twelve patriarchs and the twelve apostles. In the next windows, on either side are the twelve apostles with their insignia. St. Peter holds his keys, St. Matthew his purse, St. James, the lesser, his club, symbol of his martyrdom. Behind is St. Simon with a saw, and beside him St. Matthias who took Judas Iscariot's place. Just above and behind him is St. James the Great with a pilgrim's staff. In the opposite window St. John, the beloved disciple, wih a book, a chalice from which a serpent issues, and an eagle. By his side is St. Andrew, leaning on his cross shaped like an X, his hair and beard silvery white. Next to him is St. Bartholomew with his knife. St. Thaddeus, better known as St. Jude, stands behind him with his halberd. Above St. John is "doubting Thomas" with his building rule. The center figure is St. Philip represented with a high cross in the shape of a T. These twelve godly men are the twelve foundation stones of the restored kingdom.

Female saints are depicted in the lower part of the window. Included are St. Catherine with her wheel, St. Agnes with her lamb, St. Margaret with the cross. On the other side and opposite are St. Cecilia with her organ, St. Barbara and her tower and St. Mary with her jar of ointment.

The next windows on either side are filled with angels and archangels. Michael, Captain-General of the host of heaven, young and beautiful carries a shield and scales. By him stands Raphael, guardian angel of humanity portrayed as a pilgrim. On the right is Gabriel angel of the Annunication. By his side is Uriel, light of God. Above the angels, in fiery red, are the cherubim and seraphim who are ever round the throne of God singing "Holy, Holy Lord God."

After describing the magnificent glass panels, Mr. Huske concluded his sermon with the admonition that such a vision should make us want to conquer sin and through faith and discipline obtain our peace in the restored kingdom of God's son.

The much needed Parish House was completed in 1898 thanks to many generous gifts. The large supporters who contributed to the $25,000 outlay were the Kings, Arnolds, Morgans, Gignouxs, Winslows, Hewletts, Smiths, Childses, Eldridges, Aikers, Provosts, Miss Post, August Roesler, W.L. Stow, H.P. Booth and George B. Wilson.

The spacious new Parish House made it possible to set apart rooms for the various activities and working agencies. There was a rector's study, a choir room, a flower mission room, a sewing room, the reception hall, a dining room, a kitchen and a Sunday School room.

The next important addition to the church complex, the cloisters, was built in 1900. The family of the late August Roesler offered to build and donate the cloisters in his memory. The offer was gratefully accepted by the Vestry and by March 1901 the rectory, the parish house and the church were connected by the new cloisters.

The death of the Hon. John A. King, aged 84, occurred at this time. Not only was he a founder of All Saints Church but also well known in the diocese of Long Island. He had been one of the founders of the Missionary Society, an original incorporator of the Cathedral, nine times a delegate to the General Convention and active in the work of the Church Charity Foundation. He also founded and endowed King Hall in Washington D.C. for the higher education of Black students. He came of an old and distinguished family. His grandfather, Rufus King, was a member of the Constitutional Convention, a Senator from New York and an Ambassador to the Court of St. James. His father had been Governor of New York and he, himself, a State Senator.

Mr. Huske said of John A. King, Jr. that "of all the founders (of All Saints Church) . . . no one was more powerful in directing and developing the future character of the parish . . . His interest and loyalty are remembered by all." The Vestry held a special meeting to express their heartfelt sympathy in the loss of "our departed Senior Warden, Hon. John A. King. Years before its incorporation our parish became the object of his thoughtful solicitude and when in the fullness of time the moment came to realize his hope . . . his generosity, wisdom in counsel and patient attention to details alone made possible the firm foundation our parish has attained with its beautiful buildings and its highly developed temporal and spiritual prosperity," said the Vestry Resolution.

Bishop Littlejohn died on August 7, 1901. Services were held in the Garden City Cathedral after which he was buried in All Saints graveyard in the spot which he had chosen. A quaint and charming ceremony to commemorate the first Bishop's burial at All Saints developed in after years and is still carried out. The children of the parish bring fresh flowers to the Easter Service which are woven onto a wooden cross. After the Easter Service is over, the children march in procession, the flowery cross preceding them, to Bishop Littlejohn's grave. There prayers are said for him and for all of the All Saints clergymen who lie in the churchyard. After the brief ceremony, the children disperse to the front lawn for the annual Easter egg hunt.

In October, a special convention of the diocese was called to elect a new bishop. Messrs. Hewlett, Gignoux and Childs were elected delegates

Bishop Littlejohn's stone

from All Saints Church. The Rev. Dr. Frederick Burgess was elected second Bishop of Long Island.

The new century brought with it the promise of a bright and peaceful future for all Americans. Long Island also felt the surge of optimism and was increasing in population. Soon the railroad came to Great Neck bringing many changes especially to the lower part of the peninsula.

For All Saints Church the period was one of beautification and modernization of the physical plant. A telephone was installed in the rectory and, two years later, in 1902, the rector was empowered to arrange with the North Hempstead Light and Power Company for the installation of electric lights in the church.

In that same year, Mary Rhinelander King wrote to the vestry that she would like to place in the church, as a memorial to her parents, John A. and Mary Colden King, a carved rood screen, a pulpit, clergy and choir stalls, a carved wood reredos and "such other carvings as may be necessary to carry out the very beautiful design which was submitted to me yesterday by Mr. Silas McBee who will have the entire charge of the memorial and to whom I am most grateful."

The Vestry hastened to accept the magnificent offer. The detailed plans for the work were made by Crane, Fergus and Goodhue under the direction of Silas McBee. Craftsmen Irving and Casson carried them out exquisitely in quarter-sawed English oak with its incomparable richness of texture. "The fittings will be the finest in any church in New York and will cost a princely sum," a contemporary newspaper reported.

The Altar Saints shown as they appear in the Reredos

A detailed view of the first three Saints (left panel) Pope Gregory the Great, St. Dominic, St. Francis of Assisi

A detailed view of the center panel: St. John the Divine, The Virgin Mary, St. Joseph

A detailed view of the right panel: St. Columba, St. Augustine, St. Thomas a'Becket

The reredos contains the figures of nine saints, many of them closely associated with the history of the Anglican Church. From left to right, facing the altar, they are: Pope Gregory the Great, St. Dominic, St. Francis of Assisi, St. John the Divine, The Virgin Mary, St. Joseph, St. Columba, St. Augustine, and St. Thomas a' Becket. The reredos is built so as to form a framework and a canopy over the Sanctus windows.

All Saints Church interior before the installation of the Rood Screen

The rood screen, carved by the same craftsmen, is decorated with many Christian symbols relating to the crucifixion. In a brilliant and memorable sermon delivered sometime in the forties, Reverend Alexander McKechnie described the symbolism of the Rood Screen carvings. A series of fleur-de-lis shields can be seen on which appear the symbols of the Passion, "each of which speaks of something that happened to Him and is also a challenge to us as we strive to follow Him as He calls us to do." At the left end is a lantern representing Judas Iscariot's treachery, next a cock which stands for St. Peter's cowardice when "he cowered in darkness outside the judgment hall where Jesus was arraigned." Then come the five dice for the callous soldiers of the guard who gambled for Jesus' clothing as he suffered on the Cross. Then a cup, recalling the vinegar offered maliciously to Our Lord on the Cross. Next the robe which represents the scorn heaped upon Him. The central pair of shields show the mechanisms used in raising the Cross into position and nailing the charges in place above our Lord's head. The last five shields contain carvings of the specific objects used to torture Jesus: the three nails, the crown of thorns, the whipping post, the scourge and "the spear that drew both water and blood and so showed forth His death."

All Saints Church interior after the installation of the Rood Screen (1902)

Beneath these panels run quotations in Latin from the Nicene Creed about our Lord's Incarnation, Humanity, Suffering under Pontius Pilate, Burial, Resurrection and Ascension. Finally, just above the central archway is the Lamb of God "flanked by the symbols of the two branches of the Anglican Church which passed on the Episcopate to the Church in the United States, the thistle of the Scottish Church and the Rose of the Church of England." The base of the screen is a series of panels carved in Linen Fold which represents the linen which Our Lord wore during his Ministry on earth, in which His body was wrapped when entombed and which He wore in His appearances after the Resurrection. The delicate tracery that connects these representations is made up of carvings of the Vine, the Thorns and the Pomengranate leaf. Small angel faces peep out from the ends of the pilasters that frame the sections of the screen.

A detailed view of the top of the Rood Screen

At the top of the screen, in the center, stands a cross with figures of the Virgin Mary and St. John the Divine on either side of it. The rood screen is supported by two columns containing niches in which are statues of the Archangels Michael and Gabriel.

A detailed view of the Archangel Gabriel in the niche on the left of the Rood Screen

A detailed view of the Archangel Michael in the niche on the right of the Rood Screen

At the same time that the reredos and the rood screen were unveiled, a carved altar, in memory of the first Bishop of Long Island, was presented by the All Saints Church congregation. The altar was so dedicated in recognition of the trust committed to the worshippers at All Saints to guard Bishop Littlejohn's mortal remains.

The possibility of increasing the fees for pew rentals faced the Vestry at this time. Because of a deficit of $700 in the parish running expenses, the suggestion was made to meet the deficit by raising the rent of the front pews from $50 per year to $100 and the side pews from $25 per year to $75. A committee was appointed to study the issue. After hearing the report and debating it, the Vestry agreed with the committee's recommendations to raise th pew rentals and came up with a schedule of costs to take effect on November, 1902. Notices were to be sent to the parishioners informing them of the new fees.

Then, at the November Vestry meeting, the Rector reported that many of the church members objected to raising the pew rent. He said, also, that he had been given $2,353 and estimated that he could easily raise $4,000 more if the pews in the Church were to be made free. Mr. Huske added that "he earnestly hoped the Vestry would declare the pews to be free." The Vestry responded enthusiastically to the request and unanimously resolved that all pews should hereafter be free. Thus the Great Neck Church took the lead in this democratic movement for free pews, an action that was much applauded in the Village and resulted in greatly increased contributions to the church.

Contributions to finish the church appointments came in regularly. In 1903, money was given to redecorate the interior of All Saints and to erect a screen in the vestibule that would be in keeping with the chancel carvings and to carpet.

During the same year, George Hewlett resigned as warden and H. C. Childs was elected unanimously to be the new warden. Silas McBee was elected a vestryman.

The church tower was remodeled in 1904, at the request of Roswell Eldridge, to make room for a new set of chimes and the chimney clock. Each of the four faces of the tower had a window with wooden tracery, open without louvers, in order to allow the passage of sound from the bells. The walls of the new belfry stage were half timbered to conform with the rest of the church and the other buildings. In order to avoid the appearance of a great increase in the height of the tower, the arched tops of the four windows rise above the lines of the eaves and are crowned by half-timbered dormers. The roof is a simple pyramidal spire.

There is a clock dial on three faces of the tower made of open wrought iron placed immediately in front of the tracery in the tops of the windows which were especially designed in ivy leaf pattern by the Tiffany company.

The chiming stand and the clockworks were placed upon a gallery in the story below the belfry stage. A new flight of carved oak stairs from the baptistry (at the rear of the church) to the chiming rooms afforded easy access. The total height of the new tower corresponds exactly to the old one.

The chimes, eleven bells manufactured by Meneely & Co., West Troy, New York, were installed on May 7, 1904 with impressive ceremonies. The chimer for the inauguration, F.P. Lotz of Watervliet, New York, delighted the people with a program of secular music on Saturday and psalms and hymns on Sunday.

On July 22, 1904, the New York *Herald Tribune* carried an amusing article about the new churchbells. Summer residents of the colony who lived in the vicinity of "the stately and historic old All Saints Episcopal Church,", it said, were complaining about the bellringing of John Scott who was described as an aged Englishman who said that he once rang the chimes in Westminster Abbey. Perhaps, but, they insisted, the sounds that emanated from the stately old belfry of All Saints in the early morning resembled those of an amateur brass band. The harassed residents claimed that they were being awakened each morning by the sound of the Angelus which John tolled at a quarter to six. Then, with painful regularity, he tolled "The Blue Bells of Scotland" for two bars then "The Holy City" followed by "I'd Leave My Happy Home For You." It was rumored that the summer visitors were planning to finance a replacement for Scott.

However tongue in cheek the article was, on December 18, 1904, the Vestry engaged Fred Thurston, a parishioner, to be the chimer at $60 per year. Morgan Thurston, Fred Thurston's son who succeeded him as chimer, reported that Mr. Eldridge arranged a series of lessons for his Dad in New York City. Morgan Thurston said that many years back while driving through Troy he asked about the old bell foundry and had pointed out to him an old crumbling building. In 1978 when he returned again there was no longer any sign of it.

A set of three windows, representations of the Nativity, the Crucifixion and the Descent of the Holy Ghost at Pentecost, were unveiled on November 20, 1904. Clarkson Cowl gave them in loving memory of his mother Mary Yeoman Clark who died in 1902.

In 1906, the Church received a gift from Mary R. King of a house situated on the corner of Middle Neck and Redbrook roads called "Manilla." Miss King purchased the house to prevent the establishment of a saloon there and, in the deed presented to the Church, made the restriction that the "sale of liquor thereon is forever forbidden."

To get a picture of a typical Annual Parish Meeting of this period, let us look at the 1906 meeting, which took place during the twentieth year of the church's life. It was held, as always, on Easter Monday in the Vestry room of All Saints immediately after the morning service. The polls were opened at 9 A.M. for an hour and six ballots were cast. The results were the election of Wardens H.C. Childs and John Brown and Vestrymen Charles C. Gignoux. Moses R. Schenck, William H. Arnold, Silas McBee and Edgar H. Cook.

The vestry met monthly and took care of all the varied business of the Parish. For example, in July, a committee was appointed by the Rector to have water supplied to both buildings and grounds and the Vestry granted Mr. Huske a month's vacation and assured the expense of his Supply.

The 20th anniversary of the incorporation of All Saints Church was celebrated on Thursday, October 18, 1906 with a service of Holy Communion at 10:30 A.M. The Rt. Rev. Frederick Burgess gave an address and the Rev. C.F.H. Wrigley the anniversary sermon. After the service a luncheon was given for the guests and, from 4-7, an anniversary reception. On that Sunday, October 21, at the service of Morning Prayer, the Rector's sermon was on the history of All Saints Church. Evening Prayer had addresses by visiting clergy. The offerings of all the services were donated to the endowment fund.

The progress of All Saints Church during its first 20 years of life was very impressive. The Rector stated that it was "almost unparalleled in the diocese, and an exception outside." On this anniversary he hoped to complete the Church's endowment fund of $20,000 to "keep evergreen the hallowed graves where lie her blessed dead." Probably no founder foresaw "the present ideal parish with its dignified activities and earnestness," he commented. A summary of some statistics revealed 170 families associated with the parish, 580 baptized persons, 235 communicants. The Sunday School which started in 1895 with about 50 students now had about 200.

A contemporary newspaper noted that though only 20 years old, All Saints Church had a large membership, superb grounds and buildings worth nearly a quarter of a million dollars. It is "one of the most beautiful groups of ecclesiastical buildings in this country," the newspaper wrote, and, other than the Roman Catholic Church, the only regularly conducted denominational institution of worship in the Great Neck community.

Gifts to complete the interior of the Church and Parish House continued to be offered. Mrs. Emma Winslow gave the pipe organ from her Great Neck house to be placed in the Parish House as a memorial to her husband. J.P Van Derven was given permission to proceed with the execution of a window in memory of his mother, Augusta Emily Van Derven, to be placed over the main entrance. The Vestry had requested certain changes in the details of the plans which he agreed to have carried out. The window depicts the boy Jesus in the Temple instructing the teachers.

Psalm 121–"I will lift up mine eyes unto the hills from whence cometh my help." A Tiffany Window designed by Edward P. Sperry, 1907

Mr. Paulding Farnham gave a beautiful window in memory of his mother, Mrs. Julia Farnham. It is an exquisite example of Tiffany glass designed by Edward P. Sperry of New York, one of the Tiffany Company's most gifted artists. The window is a rendition of the 121st Psalm, "I will lift up mine eyes unto the hills, from whence cometh my help."

The Great Neck League property, which had been given to the church earlier by Mrs. Silas McBee, was sold in June, 1907 for $12,000 to W. Gould Brokaw. Under the agreement with Mrs. McBee, the proceeds of the sale was added to the endowment fund.

Mrs. George Holt presented the large triple window in the west end of the church as a memorial for her late husband. The subject is the enthroned Christ and is executed in English glass by Heaton, Butler and Baine through their American agents, the Gorham Co. of New York.

Warden John Brown, who had been a charter member of the Vestry, died in December, 1909. The superintendent of the Messenger estate, he was known familiarly as "Farmer Brown." The Vestry resolution read: "To think of him is to recall his striking figure, his strong personality, his sturdy Scotch ancestry, his genial, cordial friendly Scotch characteristics."

In 1910, Charles C. Gignoux tendered his resignation as Treasurer of All Saints Church because of ill health and his absence from Great Neck. The Vestry accepted his resignation with great regret. Dr. John H. Eden was elected unanimously to succeed him.

That same year the church sustained another major loss when Harris Caleb Childs, warden since 1904, died in December. The vacancy was filled by Dr. Silas McBee, the noted editor of *The Churchman*. His letter of acceptance came dated March 17, 1911, Jerusalem. The Senior Warden at the time was Moses R. Schenck.

Roswell Eldridge resigned from the Vestry in December, 1912. Before he left, Silas McBee moved the renewal of the agreement between Mr. Eldridge and the Vestry that the window in the gable and the door in the west of the church should never be filled with stained glass. The motion was carried as there was general acceptance that this restriction preserved better lighting in the church.

The celebration of the twenty fifth anniversary of "the handsomest edifice in the Long Island diocese," as the North Hempstead *Record* described All Saints Church, was open to the public. Mr. Huske said that invitations will be sent only to friends out of town. Every individual of the Great Neck community should consider himself invited. He hoped that everyone would take an interest in the celebration and come to show their good will and cordial Christian feelings.

Bishop Burgess officiated at the Holy Communion service at 7:30 A.M. All Saints Day, November 1, 1912. At the 11 A.M. Anniversary service, the Rev. Louis DeCormis, "who ministered to the infant organization a quarter of a century ago," gave the sermon. He spoke of the struggle the handful of people had endured 25 years earlier to organize the church and congratulated the Rev. Huske and his flock on the progress that they had made since the founding.

Under the direction of Mrs. Howard F. Clark, the church was decorated with chrysanthemums and autumn leaves brought from the gardens and greenhouses of the worshippers.

For the anniversary reception, given from 3:30-6:30 at the Parish Hall, Mrs. Roswell Edridge and her committee had transformed the hall into "a miniature Arcadia of repose and pastoral delight" with a profusion of potted palms, chrysanthemums and autumn leaves. The stage was arranged to enclose the musicians in a cosy woodland bower in front of which was placed hundreds of the rarest and choicest chrysanthemums. At the opposite end was an enthronement of palms. The guests were enchanted.

At the start of 1913, the Vestry made an important investment decision. They would place one third of the church funds in mortgages, one third in securities approved for savings bank investments and one third in other approved securities.

At the Annual Parish Meeting, held as usual on the morning of Easter Monday, the Vestry announced another important change. The next Annual Parish Meeting would be held in the evening to make it possible for more members of the congregation to attend. At that time, only male members of the congregation were entitled to vote or to become vestry members.

At the end of 1913 a gift was received that was to make a major change in the development of All Saints Church. The Vestry received a deed from Mrs. William R. Grace for certain lands in Thomaston for the erection of a chapel. The property , which was in the vicinity of Station Road and Grace Avenue and included 150 feet on Grace Avenue, was given in fulfillment of a promise made by Mrs. Grace to her husband to give the land for that purpose. The vestry accepted the offer with a vote of thanks to the donor. However, it was not until 1915 that the Rector appointed a committee to report on the advisability of building a chapel and getting architectural plans.

Dr. Louis DeCormis, All Saints Church's first rector, died in 1916. The Vestry resolution spoke of gratitude for the foundations that Rev. DeCormis had laid and his wholehearted cooperation in the establishment of the parish. "There are those in Great Neck who will never cease to rejoice in having been served by him in all the sacred relations of life," the resolution read. In her acknowledgment of the Vestry's remarks, Dr. DeCormis' daughter wrote that her father "looked upon his rectorship at Great Neck as embracing the happiest years in his ministry."

In April (1916), the parish celebrated the twentieth anniversary of the Rev. Huske's rectorship at All Saints Church. The ladies of the parish prepared a very attractive celebration. The rector asked the clerk of the Vestry to thank the ladies of the parish for their cordial assistance on the occasion of his celebration commenting on "the wonderful spirit of

A pageant celebrating the 20th year of Rectorship of the Rev. Kirkland Huske, April 25, 1916

cooperation that has always existed in the Parish." Warden McBee's motion at the May 8th Vestry meeting that the ladies be thanked for their cordial assistance in the Huske reception was the first mention of the women of the church in the vestry minutes.

At the 1917 Annual Parish Meeting, which, despite the earlier resolution, was still taking place on Easter Monday morning, Wardens Schenck and McBee were unanimously elected as were 5 vestrymen.

Prior to the Annual Meeting, in March, All Saints Church again became one of the first to accept church administrative reform. The Vestry agreed to accept an assessment to share in the support of aged and disabled clergymen and of the families of deceased clergymen. The amount payable to the Church Penison Fund was set at 7½% of the salaries paid to the clergy.

Dr. John Eden, treasurer and vestryman for many year, died in May, 1919. "A tender sympathy and unfailing patience to those in sickness, suffering or sorrow, softened and sweetened his character," the Vestry resolution said. "Unselfishness and devotion marked to a full degree his service to his Church which he loved."

The All Saints Choir about 1917–Rev. Huske at the extreme right

In October, the Vestry Music Committee which had heretofore only the Rector on it added two vestry members. One of their first acts was to thank William G. Genner, the organist, for his faithful services. However, not long afterward, Genner, who had been at All Saints for twelve years, resigned owing to the pressure of other duties. He agreed to stay until a successor could be found.

Lightning hit the church and the tower on August 31, 1920. The large Holt memorial window in the west end of the church was badly damaged also, but the insurance company, which paid for the other damage, refused to cover the stained glass. A a result the amount of insurance carried on the church was doubled.

The erection of a chapel on the Grace Avenue property became a major focus of interest to the Vestry at this time. In April, 1921, the Vestry adopted the resoltuion that, since the Rector had received $12,400 in pledges and cash and promises of other substantial help for the erection of an All Saints Church Chapel, the Vestry sanctioned the committee of the whole to take such initiative as necessary to raise the money and build the chapel. Walter Wood Parsons was made the treasurer of the chapel fund with authority to pay the needed amount for the erection

Interior of All Saints Chapel (St. Paul's)

of the chapel. Mann & McNeille of New York City were chosen to be the architects and the building contract went to George V. Bullen of Great Neck.

Later in the year, the family of Paul Brorstrom gave All Saints Church a deed for 15 feet on Grace Avenue east of the chapel. The consideration for the bequest was that its recipient love and care for a Liberty oak growing on the land that had been planted by the Brorstroms on Armistice Day, 1918. The Vestry accepted the gift with its stipulation.

By the end of 1923, thanks to the many gifts that had been donated to it, the Chapel was finished enough to hold its first service there. A debt

An Easter Sunrise Service during the Huske ministry

of $10,000, still owed on the chapel building, disturbed the Rector who wished to have it paid as soon as possible. To help defray the debt, the Vestry decided to use the Easter Offerings of both church and chapel for that purpose.

On June 10, 1923, the Rt. Rev. Frederick Burgess, Bishop of Long Island, laid the cornerstone of All Saints Church Chapel. Shortly afterwards, the Rev. William Grime, who had been the Assistant at Christ Cathedral, Hartford, was called to become the Vicar of the Chapel. A committee of prominent church members from both Church and Chapel welcomed Mr. and Mrs. Grime on their arrival in Great Neck.

In September, 1923, Mr. Huske called a special Parish Meeting to introduce two significant changes in the operation of the church for consideration. The first was an increase of the number of the vestrymen from seven to twelve to take care of the added responsibilities that the maintenance of the chapel would require. The second was a change in the date of the Annual Parish Meeting from Easter Monday to the first Monday following the first Sunday in Advent. Both measures were approved.

All Saints Church was becoming an increasingly important presence in the community. Its sunrise Easter Service was an annual celebration that was very well attended by people from all around the county. The Rector said that participants "looked forward to taking part in this unusual way of opening our day of worship to the Risen Lord." The service started promptly at 6 A.M. with the choir singing in the church tower. A number of old parishioners, to this day, when asked about their childhood recollections of All Saints Church recalled first the wonder of that Easter Service and the profusion of beautiful flowers with which the church was adorned.

The spring of 1924, due to severe illness, Mr. Huske was relieved of all his parochial cares and responsibilities. The Vestry granted him six months leave with the fervent hope that his health would be restored. In the interim, the Rev. William Grime, the Assistant, took over his duties.

The Church sustained a sad loss in the fall of 1924 when word came from Charleston, S. Carolina that their beloved warden, Silas McBee was dead. He had been a distinguished and active Episcopalian, the editor of *The Churchman* for many years and the founder of *the Constructive Quarterly*, a periodical devoted to Christian unity. He had also been a three times lay deputy to the General Convention and Vice President of the Laymen's Missionary Movement, a trustee of Sewanee and the author of *Eirenic Itinerary*.

In their tribute to him, the Vestry wrote of Dr. McBee –"For twenty years as Vestryman and Warden, Dr. McBee gave of the richness of his intellect and experience as a Catholic Churchman." Walter Wood Parsons was elected Warden to fill the vacancy.

The Vestry was very burdened with the responsibility of managing the finances and the business of both the Church and the Chapel. In October, 1924, they purchased two lots adjoining the chapel property owned by Paul Brorstrom for the erection of a vicarage on the corner of Gilchrist Road and Grace Avenue. The Vestry also agreed, after much discussion, to pay the final bill to the architects of the chapel.

The 1924 Annual Parish Meeting met, as decided, on the evening of December 1st and elected additional vestry members. In order to stagger future election properly, 4 vestrymen were elected for 3 years, 4 for 2 years and 4 for one year.

The building of the chapel vicarage was the vestry's next major endeavor. The building cost was estimated at $25,000 but only $17,500 had been pledged. However, the Vestry agreed that it was necessary to begin the work immediately or else the community would begin to lose faith in the chapel movement and so decided to authorize construction and to sign contracts not exceeding $25,000.

George Hewlett, the first warden of the parish along with John A. King, died at his home in Smithtown Branch, L.I. in April, 1925. He had been largely responsible for the fundraising necessary to meet the requirement of the deed gift for the church land. Many of the stones used for the building were cut and finished on his place and his efforts and devotion contributed an inestimable amount to the beauty of the grounds surrounding the church and cemetery.

The 30th anniversary of Mr. Huske's tenure at All Saints Church was celebrated with a reception on April 13, 1926 with the Bishop and Mrs. Stires present. Mrs. Eldridge supervised the decoration of the parish house, the Vestry financed the music and the ladies of the parish provided the refreshments. Warden Walter W. Parsons presented the Rector with several bonds as a token of affection from his parishioners and appreciation for his long and faithful service.

Easter of the same year, Henri Bendel presented to the Church an elegant set of white altar hangings embroidered in white and gold which had been made in Paris under his personal supervision. J.H. Ballantine presented a very handsome set of altar linen of an exquisite embroidered design.

A fire broke out in the Parish House basement on the night of May 8, 1926 but the quick action of the Rector, Edward Macrum, the organist, and John Brown, Jr., a choir member prevented any serious damage to the building. Macrum and the Rector were in Mr. Huske's study discussing the Sunday service. Brown was waiting in the outer rooms for the organist when he heard noises in the basement. He started downstairs and saw flames in the furnace room. He shouted for help which brought the Rector and the organist running. The three men rushed into the furnace room, fought the fire for half an hour and put it out. The Rector was burned slightly. The damage was estimated at about $100. Fortunately a fine library donated by Mary R. King which was near the place of the fire was not touched.

In March, 1927, Mr. and Mrs. William S. Barstow presented the Church with $10,000 in Metropolitan Edison Co. 5% bonds to be applied to the Endowment Fund for current expenses. They hoped that their gesture would influence others to see that church funds were put on such a basis as to place the parish "beyond the exigencies of time and chance."

The South entrance of the Church before the Porte-Cochere

The South entrance of the Church after the Porte-Cochere was built

By Easter, all the indebtedness of the Chapel was paid. On Friday, May 20, 1927 at 4:30 P.M., the Rgt. Rev. Ernest M. Stires, Bishop of Long Island, visited the parish and consecrated the chapel. After the service, the ladies of the chapel served a lovely tea on the vicarage lawn.

A stone porte-cochere extension to the church was dedicated before the regular 11 o'clock service on September 18, 1927. It was donated by Grace Hewlett in memory of her father, mother and sister.

A Yearbook and Church Directory of All Saints Parish 1887-1927 was published to commemorate forty years of "active zealous missionary and parochial activities in a rural Long Island District." Included in the pamphlet was an historical sketch written by the Rector, a description of church activities and a list of the communicants and the contributors to the church and chapel.

In the spring of 1929, the Vestry unanimously approved the Rector's offer to the congregation of Temple Bethel, Great Neck to use the meeting room in the Parish Hall for Friday evening worship while their synagogue was being built. A notice in Temple Bethel's Bulletin of April, 1929 announced that Rabbi David Goodis would hold "Services every Friday Evening at 8:30 at the All Saints Parish House." This was the earliest recorded example of ecumenical brotherhood, a policy for which All Saints Church has ever since been a pioneer.

The William and Francoise Barstow fund, established in June, 1929, was a munificent gift of $100,000 for the establishment of a Rector's retirement fund. The Vestry's motion of acceptance commented on "the far reaching benefits that must accrue to All Saints parish through the years to come by the operation of this princely endowment."

At the same June 20th meeting, the Vestry approved the appointment of the Rev. Alexander R. McKechnie as the summer Supply. Sadly, however, Mr. Huske died while on vacation. The funeral took place on July 12.

The thirty-three year rectorship of Mr. Huske at All Saints Church covered a period of time that witnessed the change from the horse and carriage days to the automobile age. During his ministry the Church grew in power and influence. Some of his notable achievements included the completion of All Saints Chapel, a large increase in the endowment fund, the addition of many beautiful memorials and acquisitions such as the cloisters, stained glass windows, the Parish House organ and the portal. Mr. Huske had also served on the standing committee and as a clerical deputy to the General Convention.

The Vestry decided to present the family of their late Rector, the Reverend Kirkland Huske, with a deed for a plot in All Saints cemetery.

3

MATURITY: The Ministry of Alexander McKechnie

The All Saints Vestry was now faced with the task of choosing a new spiritual leader. After careful consideration, at its October 3, 1929 meeting, they decided to appoint Mr. Grime, Vicar of the parish, the Rector and Mr. McKechnie, the temporary supply at All Saints, the Vicar. However, this arrangement lasted only a very short period of time.

At the same meeting, the Vestry was presented with a petition, signed by five members of the Vestry, requesting that the corporation consent to a separation of the Chapel from All Saints parish and, having done so, to deliver the deed of the Chapel property to the newly named corporation. The request was referred to a special meeting called for October 17, 1929.

The special meeting to consider the separation of church and chapel was held on the 17th as agreed. A formal request was read to the Vestry stating that it was the belief of the petitioners that "the time has come when the best interests of the Church, and of the members of the Church who attend and are identified with the Chapel, that a separation should take place and the Chapel be raised into a separate Parish. In this opinion we are, we believe, supported by those who regularly attend the services in the Chapel, and who send their children to the Sunday School to the number of three hundred." The Vestry was informed further that Bishop Stires had given verbal consent and approval to the separation. The

The Rev. Alexander McKechnie, Third Rector of All Saints Church

Wardens and Vestry of the Church were asked to give their consent and to deliver the deed of the Chapel property to the new church corporation as soon as legally possible.

The new church corporation was ready to assume the $7,250 mortgage and the notes of $4,000 owed to the Skinner Organ Co. They were also ready to pay all expenses for the running of the new church starting on the first of the month after the organization of the new church corporation.

The All Saints Church Vestry, although with some misgivings on the part of some of the Vestry members, agreed to the separation. They also generously offered to continue the privilege of purchasing plots at All Saints Cemetery to parishioners of the chapel for one year.

By May, 1930, All Saints Chapel was incorporated as St. Paul's Church, Great Neck, L.I. The Vestry of All Saints expressed its deep regret that it was necessary to sever "our most pleasant relations with the members of the chapel committee and that they would always have our sincere affection and earnest prayer." The Vestry also presented the altar which had been temporarily placed in the Chapel by the Church to St. Paul's "with the blessing of All Saints Church."

More change came swiftly. The Rev. William Grime resigned from All Saints Church to take effect June, 1930 in order to become the Rector of St. Paul's Church. When All Saints Chapel was founded in 1926, Mr. Grime had been appointed the Vicar. The tiny congregation which began with a meager handful of parishioners had grown to 350 souls. The Chapel which had been dependent on All Saints Church, now had reached its birthright as St. Paul's Church. All this had been accomplished under the leadership of its Vicar. Therefore it was fitting that the Rev. William Grime should be the first Rector of St. Paul's Church.

The Rev. Alexander McKechnie was appointed priest-in-charge of All Saints Church to fill the vacancy left by Mr. Grime but, by September, the Suffragan Bishop sent the message that, if possible, the rectorship should be filled. The Vestry complied. After a general discussion, the Rev. Alexander McKechnie was nominated by Col. Dwight. No further names were offered and Mr. McKechnie was unanimously elected the new rector of All Saints Church.

Since Mr. McKechnie had been fulfilling the Rector's duties already, the transition was very smooth. Hugh McAmis, who had been engaged as organist during that eventful October 3, 1929 vestry meeting, was continued as organist and choirmaster.

The 1930 Annual Parish Meeting of November, 1930 was of special significance for the women of the parish. The Vestry recommended that the qualifications for voting at the annual meeting be changed to include all women belonging to the parish who have the same qualifications as the men qualified to vote. The proposal was unanimously accepted. And in February, 1931, the certificate for qualification of voters was duly filed with the County Clerk's office.

The parish became nostalgically aware of the winds of change in the Spring of 1931. The old horse sheds, a relic of the church's past, were torn down and a garage addition to the rectory building was added

At about the same time, the cemetery property was enlarged by a 4.666 acre addition given by Francoise and William S. Barstow. The addition included land immediately adjoining the cemetery to the east as well as land occupied by the roadway along the southerly side of the Rectory from Middle Neck Road to the eastern boundary of Redbrook Road and from Middle Neck Road to the eastern boundary of the present cemetery. This gift was in fulfillment of a promise that had been made to Miss Elise Gignoux. Approximately 700 new burial plots would be added as a result of the bequest.

At the end of 1932, the special Committee on Policies and Programs gave an important report on the state of the Church. It examined, for example, the effect of St. Paul's separation from All Saints Church which had resulted in the withdrawal of certain financial support without a proportional reduction in expenses. The Committee concluded that, in the coming years, a comprehensive program of interest must be developed if the Parish was not to become even more dependent than it already was on special gifts for its existence. The Committee said that individual interest in the church is developed when a person is given a job to do and an active part to play. Among other suggestions recommended by the Committee were: the various guilds must attract new members, the sale of cemetery plots must be stimulated, full use must be made of church music as publicity, contact must be made with the new families in the parish, and vestry members must be available in the rear of the church on Sundays to talk to both parishioners and strangers. In addition, they recommended that a news letter be published at least three times a year to keep the membership aware of parish activities.

On Dec. 18, 1932, the New York *Times* ran an article and a picture on the All Saints Church's Christmas Eve Candlelight program. This service is regarded by the parishioners as a "feature event of the church year" and looked forward to and attended in large numbers, the newspaper reported. The article emphasized the excellence of the musical offerings. It said that Hugh McAmis, organist and choirmaster, had rehearsed the choir of 25 voices, selected especially for the occasion, in a program of representative Christmas carols.

The All Saints Choir in the 1930's - Rev. McKechnie at the extreme right

Times were hard for the church as they were for the nation in the era of the great depression. The Vestry Budget Committee tried to do two things to help the situation: to make a fair estimate of the revenue and to make recommendations of expenditures for the operation of the church within these limits. William S. Barstow made an important statement on the obligation of the parishioner to his church in a report to the vestry in October, 1933. It is as significant now as it was then and it was made by one of the most generous and enduring of the All Saints Church benefactors. He commented: "I have often heard it said that you cannot shut down a church. This is only partly true. While no individual is able to accomplish this, a group of individuals by declining to contribute to its support, accomplishes this very end."

William Wood Parsons died on July 29, 1934. He had been clerk of the Vestry for 12 years and Junior Warden since 1924. It was largely due to his vision and untiring efforts in the face of meager encouragement that the plan of the Reverend Kirkland Huske to build All Saints Chapel, now St. Paul's Church, was accomplished, the Vestry Resolution said.

Building the new Parish House (Huske Memorial), north side

The Barstows at this time, offered to provide an endowment fund of $20,000 to build a new church school to be known as the Kirkland Huske Memorial. In a letter, Barstow said, "appreciating that a Sunday School is a vital contributing factor to the successful growth of a parish," two years ago he had engaged a prominent architect to prepare several plans. The plans included classrooms, a large auditorium, a modern kitchen, a boiler room and a heating plant.

The Vestry, very pleased with the Barstow proposal, voted to add the bequest of $2,555.63 from the estate of Mrs. Silas McBee to the Kirkland Huske Memorial Fund. And, at the Annual Parish Meeting, a resolution was passed unanimously thanking Mr. and Mrs. William S. Barstow "for their splendid generosity and vision in providing so beautiful and complete a memorial to our late beloved Rector, the Rev. Kirkland Huske," and assuring the donors that "we will further the work."

In addition to their gift of the Kirkland Huske Memorial, the Barstows offered to provide the auditorium with a pipe organ and an endowment

Building the new Parish House (Huske Memorial), south side

for its maintenance. And, on May 5, 1935, the Kirkland Huske Memorial Parish House was dedicated by the Rt. Rev. Ernest M. Stires, Bishop of Long Island.

In October, Hugh McAmis, the church organist, gave an organ recital on the Frederic Duclos Barstow memorial organ at the new parish house to a packed audience. An alms basin was placed near the entrance for those who wished to contribute to the music fund. The stage was banked with palms and a basket of magnificent chrysanthemums stood on the organ. The well balanced program was enhanced by dramatic lighting effects.

A ten-year resident of Great Neck, who signed himself "Pater Familias," wrote a letter to the Great Neck *Record* (Sept. 27, 1935) describing his feelings about All Saints Church. He said that "the congregation is small — all too small — but a happier group of or one more devoted to their church and rector would be hard to find. The church itself and churchyard with its quiet cemetery is one of extreme loveliness growing more so as it mellows with the years. The familiar music is beautiful and inspiring and the word of God, as expounded by our eloquent rector has a direct and real meaning which goes home with me and helps me all week in a thousand ways."

The first vestry meeting of 1936 opened with a memorial prayer for the life and work of Moses R. Schenck, senior warden. A telegram from W.S. Barstow was read which spoke of Mr. Schenck's "fearless honesty and noble character." The Vestry's letter to Mrs. Schenck said that Moses R. Schenck has given us an exceptional example of simple, unfaltering faith in God and loyalty to his Church. . .a faithful communicant, teacher and officer of the Church School for 40 years, vestryman for 13 years, warden for 25 years."

A special vestry meeting was called in March to consider the problem of a very limited income which reduced considerably the allotment to the Buildings and Grounds Committee. It was decided that in the event of an increase in receipts, the Buildings and Grounds Committee would get first priority because of the danger of deterioration if the buildings were neglected. In the meantime, the work that was needed immediately such as repair of leaks, leaders, slates and gutters would be done.

Response to letters sent by the Cemetery Committee asking for trees and shrubs for planting the cemetery grounds was very gratifying. Mrs. R.C. Hall gave ten pink dogwoods, Mrs. R.N. Church gave 30 dogwood shrubs and Mrs. Roswell Eldridge gave 40 trees and 100 or more shrubs.

In the fall, Mr. Gignoux, accompanied by Col. Dwight and Mrs. Schermerhorn, went through his woods and selected 32 trees which he had root-pruned and readied for transplanting to the cemetery grounds. Mr. Schermerhorn also visited Mrs. Eldridge's nurseries and selcted 300 shrubs to be moved to the cemetery as a gift from her. By December, the Cemetery Committee was able to report that the plantings were completed and that additional planting of trees from Mr. Gignoux's woods would be done in the spring.

On All Saints day, 1936, the opening of the Golden Jubilee Year, the Recessional Hymn used in the Church's All Saints Day services of 1886 and 1887 was sung: "Who are these like stars appearing/There before God's throne who stand?/Each a golden crown is wearing/Who are all this glorious band?/Alleluia! Hark they sing/Praising loud their heavenly King."

During the year of the Golden Jubilee, Robert A. Ellard was elected Junior Warden. In May, the Woman's Auxiliary gave a series of garden parties that were very well attended and successful as was the annual Strawberry Festival held on June 18th.

Bishop Stires was present at the 50th Anniversary service to which neighboring churches had been invited. The music was so outstanding that Bishop Stires commended the choir as one of the finest on Long Island. Refreshments for the Jubilee reception had been prepared by the

Vestry wives and generous donations for the reception were made by Mr. Levitt and Mrs. Eldridge.

The Barstows concern and generosity to the Church was unceasing. They added a room to the organist's apartment in the Memorial Building and presented plans and sketches to the Vestry for a Receiving Vault to be used for winter interments. A few months later the Barstows financed repairs to the Memorial Building and the Rectory. And, in September, 1938, they had iron gates with stone posts erected at the lower roadway. By November, both the Receiving Chapel and the Gateway were completed. Bishop Stires dedicated them both at a special service after which the Barstows were presented with an illuminated testimonial.

At the 1939 Annual meeting, which took place on December 1st, Mr. McKechnie was pleased to report the addition of 53 new families to the parish. He also announced some reforms to be instituted in election proceedings and called attention to the splendid work that Mrs. Edwards, the assistant organist, had done with the junior and intermediate choirs and the probationers.

War in Europe seemed to have no effect on the pattern of social and fund raising events that constituted church activities until in June, 1940, Mr. Stockley addressed the Vestry. He said, "Due to the serious conditions that confront our country today and the necessity for preparedness," the church should not fail to do its part. It must be a moving spirit in the community taking the lead in bringing home to the people in the parish that this country is practically helpless in a military and possibly other ways. He suggested a service "of a true patriotic nature," for bringing home this truth and also for promoting confidence and courage and hope for the future. The Vestry, agreeing with his sentiments, chose to hold such a service at 11 o'clock on Sunday, June 23rd.

A Book of Remembrance was set up in November, 1940, to record all of the memorial gifts made to the parish from the time of the first cash bequests. The income from this fund would be available to replace the permanent articles in the church.

At the 1940 Annual Parish Meeting, Miss Elsie Huske offered a resolution on the occasion of the 10th anniversary of the Rector's service at All Saints Church. The resolution expressed "our heartfelt thankfulness and appreciation of the service and pastoral guidance of our Rector in the last ten years. May God give him the strength and good health to carry on."

At this time, Mrs. Roswell Eldridge requested the vestry to make a survey to see if the church might render additional service in the community. In a conversation with Mrs. Eldridge, a vestry member reported, she had suggested that the Rector should have assistance to broaden the scope of his work which would add members and mean more revenue. Mrs. Eldridge was willing to assist in the increased cost but felt that the parish should assume the greatest part of the responsibility. The vestry agreed to make such a survey.

The relative merits of hiring a full time parish secretary or a curate were debated. Mr. McKechnie pointed out the advantage of a parish secretary who would have an office on the premises from 9-4, take telephone messages and keep parish records. Mrs. Marks would continue with her part time work and Mrs. Elizabeth Frank was suggested for the full time job. Several vestry members opposed the plan considering that a curate would be of more assistance to the needs of the parish. However, in a special vestry meeting called in March, 1941, the dilemma was resolved by the decision to hire clerical assistance. Mrs. Frank, said Mr. McKechnie, was the logical person for the job because of her parish contacts through the junior choir.

The Rector asked for the cooperation of the Vestry in a roll call that was being conducted throughout the church in this country. The purpose, he explained, was "to unite Christian people in this time of crisis and to stem the tide that threatens our democratic society and our religious freedom."

In June, 1941, Mrs. Eldridge financed essential repairs and improvements to the church. Her architect, George Chappell, suggested that the green burlap in the chancel be replaced with a beige covering that would harmonize with the woodwork and produce more light and a better resonating surface. It would be necessary to suspend services in the church for 4-6 Sundays to complete the proposed work as well as necessary repairs on the organ. In September, Mrs. Eldridge offered to have the ceiling in the nave treated in the same way as that in the chancel and to put in a new floor in the chancel and the steps leading to the chancel and to change the carpeting. Her generous offers were received with thanks and gratitude.

A proposal of the Men's Activities Committee to invite some of the service men from Mitchell Field to dinner at their homes followed by evening entertainment at the Parish House was accepted eagerly by the Vestry.

The effects of the entry of the United States into World War II in December, 1941, were felt by the church almost at once. Air raid precautions required that adequate equipment for the buildings be provided. To meet the needs, Harold Kriel was appointed Air Raid Warden and a stirrup pump was purchased. The vestry spent a lot of time discussing the best procedure to follow if an alarm sounded during a church service and there were regular air raid drills conducted by the teachers and children of the church school. Requests were made to turn over the church buildings to the people in the community for refuge as well as for a first aid station. Both requests were granted. The Rector attended meetings with the many civilian defense organizations so that the church might be as useful as possible in the national emergency. The kindergarten room was turned over to the Defense Council for the duration for use as an auxiliary post. The Red Cross was granted the use of the Parish House as a place of refuge following an "All Clear" and the use of the kitchen for the canteen between the hours of twelve to four.

A service flag was dedicated and the service roster read at a service held on Nov. 8, 1942, at which Lt. Willett, a young English naval officer, was the guest organist.

The Vestry refused the resignation of Lt. Gerald B. Faigle because it had adopted the policy that all vestrymen called into the armed forces would retain their positions as active vestrymen unless membership in the Vestry was reduced below a quorum. The Vestry also decided that men who were no longer active vestrymen would become honorary vestrymen as long as they remained in the parish. This decision was commended by Bishop DeWolfe.

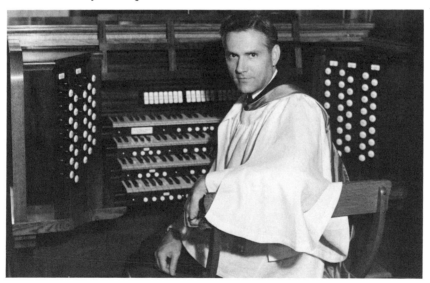

Hugh McAmis, Organist and Choirmaster at the All Saints organ

Hugh McAmis, the organist, left the parish to enlist in the U.S. Army as an Assistant Chaplain. While in training at Camp Wolpers, Texas, he became ill and died on August 18, 1942, just a few days after induction.

A Vestry resolution on the death of Hugh McAmis deplored the circumstances that caused his death. Although he had been assigned to serve as Assistant Chaplain at Camp Wolpers, McAmis was compelled to undergo the extremely rigorous basic training designed for the young selectees in spite of the protests of the Chaplain. The strain of carrying a heavy pack and marching and drilling in the hot Texas sun was more than McAmis' age and delicate constitution could endure.

The flagrancy of this case focussed attention on the inhumanity and folly of such lack of discrimination in the treatment of recruits, the Vestry statement asserted. "It is creditably stated that the unnecessary sacrifice of our dear friend has brought about a change in the rules in favor of more consideration being exercised in the training of the more elderly recruits."

A new Sunday service, directed to the needs of the families and friends of servicemen was introduced. These half hours of simple meditation on Sunday evenings were held for the duration. During each service, the names of all of the All Saints parishioners who were in the armed services were read. At this time, eighty-six names were inscribed on the All Saints Honor Roll, one of them in gold. Mr. McKechnie said of this service that he hoped a large number of worshipers would gather together for corporate prayer on these Sunday evenings in the spirit of deepening devotion to our common cause.

Many parishioners questioned how anyone could celebrate Christmas in 1942 with so many of our men and women away at war. The Rector answered these doubts with comforting and inspiring words. "As a matter of God's truth, more of the celebration of Christmas is exactly what we and all the world needs—the remembrance that the Son of God came into a distressed and harrowed world of men and women to bring life and love, spiritual power and sure faith . . . We need to celebrate Christmas, not perhaps with the merriment and hilarity of years past, but with more real joy and thankfulness that the God who comes to us also comes to our men and boys, to our women and girls, now absent from us" and "to the desolate and oppressed everywhere."

Col. Arthur Dwight started the Hugh McAmis Memorial Fund, in honor of his thirteen year service as organist and choirmaster, with a gift of five thousand dollars. The annual income from the fund was to be spent for the general maintenance of the Jane Reed Dwight Memorial Organ and any excess for expenses connected with the choir and church music. Hugh McAmis had been the first organist to use this organ, which All Saints had received in 1929. Col. Dwight wrote: "Hugh was a great musician, a charming personality, a devoted servant of our church and a loyal friend to our whole parish. His true character shone forth in his quiet acceptance of his patriotic duty to his country and the supreme sacrifice which followed so swiftly."

As the war continued, emergency measures had to be taken such as shutting down the operation of the memorial parish house except for the Sunday Church School sessions due to oil rationing. The Red Cross surgical dressing work room was moved to the old parish house and the Rector used part of the church grounds for a victory garden.

William S. Barstow died in January, 1943. The Vestry said of him that he was "a man of great vision who guided his use of his personal talents to the enrichment of the lives of thousands, and one who showed in countless known and unknown ways his sense of Christian stewardship."

Hugh McEdwards was engaged to be the new church organist. He was a member of the American Guild of Organists and former organist at the Flatbush Presbyterian Church.

In September, 1943, the Treasurer was pleased to report that the parish was in excellent financial condition. The parish Day Guild gave the music program a gift of money to cover the services of an additional tenor and bass. The Vestry complimented the Day Guild for the unprecedented success of that June's Strawberry Festival.

The war was never far from everyone's thoughts. In the fall, a special Corporate Communion in recognition of the loyalty to God and country shown by those in the service was held. At the service, which was attended by over one hundred men and boys, all of the one hundred sixty names on the All Saints Church Honor Roll were read aloud.

Mr. McKechnie appealed to the Vestry to purchase war bonds as part of the investment of church money. He also suggested that the parishioners begin a fund for the renovation of the parish house by purchasing war bonds and then donating them to All Saints. Both suggestions were received with enthusiasm.

Alvin Sinclair Bullen, who had been encouraged and supported throughout the period of his studies by the All Saints parish, was ordained to the diaconate by the Rt. Rev. James P. De Wolfe at All Saints Church on Dec. 18, 1943. After the service, the guests attended a luncheon at which a communion set was presented to the new Deacon from the Rector, Wardens, Vestry and Women's Auxiliary.

On Whitsunday, 1944, Bishop De Wolfe confirmed an exceptionally large group of children and adults. Attendance at All Saints was so high at this time that the assistance of Lt. Irving S. Pollard of the Merchant Marine Academy at the 11 o'clock Sunday service was a great help to Mr. McKechnie. The Rector's 15th Anniversary celebration was held during the All Saints octave.

V E day was celebrated joyously. After the official proclamation was made, the chimes were rung and then continued to be rung throughout the day. Prayers and thanksgiving were offered every hour on the hour and a special service with a full choir took place at 8 P.M.

A special prayer service, held at the Great Neck High School on April 22nd for the opening of the San Francisco Conference, marked the first occasion upon which all of the denominations in the community participated together. About a year later, during Brotherhood week there was a Great Neck High School Assembly at which Mr. McKechnie, Father Collins and Rabbi Rudin were the speakers.

With the war over, much thought was given to incorporating the new young couples in the community and the returning servicemen into the church fellowship. A young couples club was organized under the leadership of Mr. and Mrs. Elmer Ninesling. It was an immediate success.

On a more serious note, Mr. McKechnie became interested in the Reconstruction and Advance Fund for the rebuilding of churches that had been destroyed during the war and for the advancement of Christian work throughout the world. The Rector stressed the importance of this opportunity "to spread the Gospel of Christ to all nations" and urged that the All Saints parish be very liberal in its support. The speaker at the Annual Parish Meeting discussed the Reconstruction and Advance Fund so effectively that the Vestry voted to participate in it and to conduct a canvas for it during the winter.

The increase in church membership and the need for involving the younger men in church work led to a proposal of an "Associate Vestry." Each vestry committee would have one or two such non-vestrymen on it. This was especially necessary, its advocates argued, if there was to be a rotating vestry. A meeting was planned for all interested men although some vestry members objected to the term, "Associate Vestrymen." After a good deal of discussion and thought, the scheme was adopted with the new organization to be known as the "Auxiliary Vestry." Its primary duties were clearly defined: zoning the parish, making annual parish visits, ushering, scouting and handling publicity. It was agreed that the Auxiliary Vestry would be looked upon as a training ground for future vestry members.

After thirty names of possible auxiliary vestrymen were collected, each vestryman was asked to submit two choices from the list. An Auxiliary Vestry of fiteen was then appointed. It met with the Vestry for the first time in joint session in May, 1947. At the meeting, the Auxiliary Vestry presented the Vestry with a zoning map after which the entire group discussed the best way to make contact with new families.

Col. Arthur Dwight died in 1946 leaving a bequest in his will to be known as the Dwight Memorial Fund. The income from it was to be used for organ maintenance or any other work of the church connected with music.

The establishment of the United Nations in Lake Success stirred up a great deal of interest among the All Saints parishioners. They decided to invite two hundred and forty United Nations members to a get together tea which was a great success.

The 60th Anniversary of All Saints Church was celebrated with an informal reception given on Sunday evening, November 3, 1947. There were about one hundred and fifty guests including the Rector of St. George's, Hempstead, the grandparent parish, the Rector of Christ Church, Manhasset, the parent parish, the Rector of St. Paul's, the daughter parish and the Rectors of St. Stephen's, Port Washington and Trinity, Roslyn, the sister parishes. A musical program was presented.

During this period of All Saints' history, there were about four hundred and fifty pledges each year and in January of 1949, the Treasurer reported that over ninety percent of them were paid up. Social activities were many and varied and provided for all age categories such as Men's Club picnics in Kings Point Park, a costume barn dance for the couples and a picnic for the Young People's Fellowship (ages 16-21).

In 1949, once again sensitive to community needs, the Vestry approved a request from the Superintendent of Schools of Great Neck for the use of one or two rooms in the parish house for kindergarten and first grade students. A corner of the churchyard was set aside for a playground. The Vestry also granted use of the building to Alcoholics Anonymous for evening meetings.

A number of changes were made during that year that are still in effect. The church order of service program was changed to a fourpage folder so as to include notices of the special events of the following week. And the Christmas Eve service was changed to its present format of carol singing followed by a communion service.

Church statistics were very encouraging. Attendance at Sunday services, (they were at 8 A.M., 9:30 A.M. and 11 A.M.), had increased greatly from 1948 to 1949. One hundred more were in attendance at regular services nd two hundred more at the communion service.

During the summer months, vandalism in the cemetery became so serious a problem that members of the vestry and the auxiliary vestry took turns on night patról. This escalation of vandalism was particularly disturbing because during the war the State Legislature had amended the law on religious vandalism raising it from a misdemeanor to a felony.

Both vestries had a joint meeting in October, 1949 and then attended a dinner hosted by Mr. and Mrs. McKechnie. At the open meeting which followed, wives were permitted to remain for the first time.

Money was always, and perhaps inevitably, a chronic problem. Among the subjects that were controversial at the time were an Assistant for the Rector and paid singers. It was argued that an Assistant would make it possible to extend the number of parish calls made and increase the scope of the work with young people. The Vestry agreed about the advisability of an Assistant but worried about the cost. However, in regard to paid singers some of the vestrymen just wanted to eliminate the cost while others pointed out that some people attended All Saints Church because of the quality of the music. The question of hiring a curate was set aside for six months because it would take that amount of time to find one and the problem of paid singers was resolved, for the time being, by eliminating payment of their travel expenses.

Although there were five hundred and sixteen individual pledges for 1950, the percentage of payment was under ninety percent. This made for monetary problems due to the Bishop's request for an extra missionary budget to be taken in April, 1950. The slogan he had chosen for the program was "One World in Christ." The Vestry decided to send letters to the Diocesan Treasurer and to the Treasurer of the National Council registering the constructive criticism that constant and increased appeals for funds should be tempered with a little practical thinking. As a result, the Great Neck quota was reduced to half the original sum asked. In a discussion several months later, the Vestry agreed that its first and primary duty was to its own church in its own community and its needs must take precedence over any other requests from farther afield. The problem was somewhat alleviated the following year by the establishment of the Episcopal Charities of Long Island which coordinated all diocesan activities and thus eliminated constant asking by the diocese.

Gifts of all kinds were bestowed on All Saints regularly. J. Charles Frank donated a new oil burner. A legacy of fifteen thousand dollars was left by Lawrence Hill. Two silver cruets and two alms basins were given in honor of Miss A.M. Hooker. The Parish Day Guild, ever generous, gave one thousand dollars for rewiring the chancel, paid the balance due on some bills and redecorated the Rector's study.

In 1950, for the first time, auxiliary vestrymen were used to fill in as canvassers for the every member canvass. The canvass started with a meeting of twenty-nine men at the home of Morgan Grace, Jr. at which Mr. McKechnie asked that he be informed regularly of the progress of the work. He said that the greatest effort must be made not only to attract newcomers to the church but also to keep oldtimers, many of whom no longer attended services. The Rector's part would be through personal contact, the Vestry's to see that the high standards of services were maintained and that the parish operated on a sound financial basis. In summary, the whole purpose of the church is to build the Kingdom of God and everytime a canvass is conducted, the Kingdom of God is strengthened, Mr. McKechnie stated.

During its March, 1951 meeting, the vestry, in an unusually frank exchange of ideas, examined many attitudes. One member said, in answer to a request for an additional maintenance man, that the maintenance of elaborate buildings and grounds was not as important to the Episcopal Church as evangelism. The appointment of a curate came under fire. One vestryman commented that the older parishioners wanted the Rector to call on them not a curate. Another dissent was made about the church service which, a vestryman said, had changed from a single low church service to a more elaborate one. We are losing Protestants in the area, he claimed. Another vestryman asserted that All Saints was no longer the little country church of thirty or forty years ago. We have lost community, he said. We spend thirty to forty thousand dollars a year and have only fifty to sixty people at the 11 o'clock service. Mr. McKechnie answered that he made forty to sixty calls a month and could do no more. There definitely was a need for a curate who could help the church to function in all areas. The Vestry was satisfied that so many problems had been aired and agreed to speak of them again in the near future.

Confirmation Whitsunday, 1951 (partial). Bishop DeWolfe and Rev. McKechnie

After deep consideration, the Vestry decided to emply a Seminarian for an eight month period to work in the Church School with the Senior class and the Young People's Fellowship, to assist the Rector in the church and to call on families with youngsters. It was understood that he would not call on older people. The Seminarian would work all day Sunday and part of Saturday at a stipend of fifty dollars per month. The Woman's Auxiliary offered to give two hundred and fifty dollars toward the cost. George B. Wharton was hired.

At 9 A.M., February 15, 1952, All Saints Church held a memorial service for the late King George VI of England to coincide with the time of his interment. The gesture was in recognition of the Episcopal Church's tie with the Anglican Communion and the position of the English ruler as "the defender of the faith."

In March, the Rector was able to report to the Vestry that attendance at services had increased over the year and that the Young People's Fellowship was flourishing under George Wharton's leadership. The Vestry voted to continue Wharton's employment.

However, Mr. McKechnie regretted to report also that many known to be communicants left church before the celebration. He asked the Vestry, particularly the Publicity or Education Committee, to devise a way to inform the parishioners of the vital importance of receiving Holy Communion regularly.

The All Saints Thrift Shop opened its doors in 1954. The Women's Auxiliary planned it as a shop for the sale of used clothes and articles to be open every Tuesday and to yield enough money to take the place of two annual rummage sales. The Thrift Shop's success was immediate and, in no time, it needed more space.

George Wharton was unable to continue at All Saints in 1953 due to the pressure of his work at the Seminary. His place was taken by Joseph Trask, a Senior Seminarian, who was experienced in working with young people.

A coffee hour after the 11 o'clock Sunday service, a custom that has continued to the present time, was introduced in the fall of 1952 in order to "avoid the criticism that the Episcopal Church is a cold proposition." The coffee hour was held each week at the rectory with the members of the various organizations taking turns as hosts and hostesses.

Upset by the small balance with which 1953 closed, the Vestry reopened discussion on the need for a curate. The objectives defined were an increased congregation and new names on the subscription list. Mr. McKechnie again enumerated the advantages of having a curate such as supervision of all youth work, first calls on new residents to screen them for a rector's follow up and help with "release time classes." If the curate was a priest, he could do some preaching. No definite decision was made until the following year when a sum of money was earmarked for a curate's salary.

The Vestry did, however, clarify the use of The Book of Memory or Memorial Endowment Fund. Its final decision was that "it is the intention of the Book of Memory Fund that its income be unrestricted, but primarily allocated to the consecrated portion of the Church." The Rector then entered into the Book of Memory a list of all the gifts and memorials that had been made to All Saints.

Many of the activities of the Lenten season were taken over by the Auxiliary Vestry. It proposed a series of discussions on "What is an Episcopalian?", a project that proved to be very well received and very well attended by parishioners.

The Auxiliary also took over the Boy Scout troop. For a long time, All Saints had been the host of a very active troop although there had been many problems over the use and misuse of the scout room and frequent changes in scoutmasters. With the new arrangement, the difficulties ceased.

In April, 1954, a new publication, called "The Beech and the Belfry" was launched. It was a weekly newsletter whose purpose was to provide the parishioners with immediate information about church affairs.

The 25th Anniversary of Mr. McKechnie's ordination was commemorated on June 23rd. Bishop Sherman came to the 11 o'clock service which was followed by a luncheon prepared by the Women's Auxiliary.

In the fall, there were several special Sunday services. Christian Education Sunday, October 3, was the day for the parents of the students to show their appreciation of the fine work done by the Church School staff. On Laymen's Sunday, October 17, one of the Church laymen gave the address which was an appeal for the annual canvass. The following two Sundays were dedicated to the United Nations and the annual canvass. On November 1, the All Saints octave began and November 7 was All Saints Sunday. The Rector asked the Vestrymen to be present at these services to meet new residents and to encourage them to be part of the parish.

After an ardent search, the Vestry hired a new curate, Charles Baker. He was thirty-three years old and married, a former employee of Republic, a veteran of World War II and highly recommended by the Bishop. Mr. Baker was ordained a Deacon at the Cathedral in late November, 1954.

The Curate reported to the Vestry each month on the results of his calls on former and potential parishioners. In one of his reports, he summed up some of the negative comments that had been made to him. There were objections to the constant changes in position, sitting, kneeling and standing. There were objections also to lighted candles, crosses and processions. Mr. Baker said that he got favorable reactions when he explained the meaning of the usages.

The Bishop ordained Mr. Baker to the priesthood at All Saints Church in June so that he was able to take over all of the Rector's duties during Mr. McKechnie's summer vacation. The Vestry, Altar Guild and Women's Auxiliary presented the new priest with a private communion set.

At the Annual Meeting, Mr. McKechnie, reflecting on his tenure at All Saints, particularly thanked Hugh MacNair, Moses Schenck, Gilbert Stoutenburgh, Walter Parsons and Robert Ellard for their help to him. He said that when he first came there had been no parish list and the first one, prepared in 1941, showed four hundred families. Now there were approximately five hundred families, which was only a twenty-five per cent gain in twenty-five years, he admitted, but, he explained, "we are no longer the well rooted residential family parish that we were twenty-five years ago." Approximately fifty percent of the people of the parish list were "on a three year transient residency in our community." Of the original four hundred names on the parish roll, only one hundred remain. Mr. McKechnie stated that the people of the parish were showing an increasing disposition to come to the church for guidance. He also observed that, in his opinion, no man should stay on the vestry too long and that "new blood" was important.

A memorial gift received at this time was a medium sized silver cruet given by Mr. and Mrs. Pratt in memory of Elizabeth and George Hayden and used for the first time at the Christmas services. Three thousand dollars was given to the Cemetery Endowment Fund from the estate of Grace Hewlett along with a portrait of George Hewlett, All Saints Church's first warden.

In 1956, the Election Board requested the use of the parish hall for a polling place. The Vestry decided that it was its civic duty to agree to the demand and the hall is still used as a polling place.

In the spring, an analysis of attendance records showed an increase in attendance. The Rector said that this was due to calls made on parishioners by the clergy and to the work of the Auxiliary Vestry. He also complimented the curate for his work in increasing the membership of the Young Peoples Fellowship.

The parish was proud, at this time, of the election of Mr. McKechnie to the Diocesan Council.

To stimulate attendance at services during the summer, men were encouraged to come to church without a jacket and to wear an open-necked shirt, innovations that were publicized in *The Herald*. However, the liberalism was not extended to gambling. St. Paul's School asked for support of its Bazaar at which chances for a Cadillac were being sold. Mr. McKechnie ruled that this was counter to the House of Bishops directive against gambling and also against his own principles.

Mr. Baker, the curate, accepted the rectorship of St. Paul's Church, College Point, but agreed to remain at All Saints until November 1st. The Bakers were given a farewell reception at the Parish House. The annual canvass was conducted after Mr. Baker had gone but the unusually cordial welcome that the canvassers received was credited to the groundwork laid by the former curate.

Before the Annual Meeting, the Rector spoke very seriously to the Vestry about the need for "new blood" on the Vestry. He said that many parishioners had accused him or the Vestry or both of remaining a closed corporation with control of nominations. After discussion on whether the Rector should appoint a Nominating Committee or if all nominations should come from the floor, it was decided that Mr. McKechnie should select some of the most outspoken critics to serve as members of the Nominating Committee.

In December, the Rector asked the members of the Auxiliary Vestry to found a Men's Club, the Brotherhood of St. Andrew, by approaching one hundred or more male parishioners and asking them about their interests. He asked the Auxiliary also to build up the life of the parish by disproving two false criticisms that people had against the Episcopal Church. One, that it is an unfriendly church and, two, that All Saints is an unfriendly parish.

On Christmas day 1956, members of All Saints went carolling to the children's ward at North Shore Hospital and took gifts to the children.

All Saints, again without a curate, the Vestry suggested the possibility that the need for one had diminished. Mr. McKechnie answered that this was not so "as long as the parish holds to its present size." The search for a curate resulted in the appointment of James Birdsall for a one year period starting in June. He was a deacon, which meant that he could not take over when the Rector went on his summer vacation, but he expected to be ordained in six months time. Mr. McKechnie solved the problem by agreeing to be present Sundays during the summer and to take his vacation in January.

Mr. Birdsall was ordained at the Cathedral on Saturday, November 3rd. A luncheon for the Birdsall family was served by the Women's Auxiliary at the Parish House followed by a reception from four to six so that the parishioners could congratulate the new priest.

The Annual Meeting for 1957 was preceded, as it had been for many years, by a roast beef dinner held in the auditorium. During the evening,

Hugh McEdwards gave an illustrated talk on the cathedrals and churches of England and Scotland that he had visited during the summer while attending the international Convention of Organists. After attending a concert given by Mr. McEdwards in November, Bishop Sherman said that "The music on Sunday evening took us out of this world and carried us to sit in heavenly places."

Mrs. J. Edward Meyer donated a new lectern Bible in December. The old one, which had been given in honor of Mrs. Meyer's mother, had served All Saints for thirty-five years but was so worn it had to be replaced.

The varied and valuable work of the Women's Auxiliary which, year after year was done with tireless energy and devotion deserves more attention than has been given to it in these pages. Using 1957 as a typical year, the Women's Auxiliary accomplished the following (a partial list): making jewelry, pins earrings and pendants, for the Christmas Bazaar; making gifts and children's clothes for a box sent to St. Paul's Protestant Episcopal Church in Rome; presents and bandages for the Cancer Society, Christmas cheer for missions in South Dakota and Alaska and for the children of St. Mary's Hospital, Bayside; Thanksgiving baskets for Great Neck families in need, articles for Puerto Rico and layettes for the Youth Consultation Service and local hospitals. In addition, the Women's Auxiliary presented the parish office with a new mimeograph machine and new typewriter.

The problem of getting new families into the church since there were few Episcopalians moving into the community was a thorny one that was studied with care by the Rector and the Curate especially after the end of the year figures showed a downward trend in church attendance even at Christmas and Easter. But no solution was found.

There was some consternation when it became known that the village planned to widen Middle Neck Road from Arrandale Avenue to Redbrook Road which would take land away from the front of All Saints Church. However, after examination of the plans, it appeared that the widening would not damage the beauty of the church property. The plan was to build a retaining wall, no more than seven feet at its greatest height, of materials to match that of the church. But, when the final plans for the wall were completed, it became clear that the county, in order to save money, was going to use concrete instead of stone for the wall. The vestry met with Charles E. Smith, Commissioner of Public Works for Nassau County and insisted that the present stone wall must be replaced by another stone wall. Mr. Smith offered a compromise—that the county would get an estimate for stone facing and that he would present the problem to Holly Patterson. His offer was approved.

The feasibility of starting an Episcopal school at All Saints to be built on property adjacent to the church was the Vestry's major concern in 1958. The Rector, the Bishop and St. Paul's Church, Great Neck all favored the plan but then it was regarded with misgivings by some vestrymen. The dissenters asked if there was really a need for such a school, whether families in the parish could afford additional fees and how much of the Rector's and the Curate's time would be devoted to the school. The Vestry asked for a study of these issues to be followed by a report.

In time, it became apparent that to build an Episcopal school at All Saints was not practical chiefly for financial reasons. However, St. Paul's, Great Neck opened a nursery and kindergarten school. Father Norris, rector of St. Paul's, said that he expected a first year enrollment of twenty to thirty children.

Senior Warden Hugh McNair resigned from the Vestry in November. The Vestry passed a formal record of appreciation for his twenty-one years of devoted service.

Altar rails that could be closed were installed at All Saints. Geisler's first design was rejected as too ornate and too heavy but, after the design was modified by reducing the amount of scroll work to a minimum, the Vestry accepted it.

In June, 1959, the Rector announced that it was customary for the clergy to observe the official anniversaries of their ordination. Since Bishop Sherman would be at All Saints for Confirmation on the 21st, Mr. McKechnie wished to ask the Bishop for special prayers on his behalf and to accept his rededication to the priesthood.

The 1959 Annual Parish Meeting was held on Nov. 30th with the Curate, Mr. Birdsall presiding in the Rector's absence. The McKechnies were on a cruise. Instead of the customary dinner, dessert and coffee were served because it had been decided that the cost of dinner had accounted, in part, for poor attendance.

The Rector reported that the AME Zion Church on Steamboat Road was having a building program and that the Ministers and Rabbis Association of Great Neck and other service organizations had endorsed the program. The Vestry voted to give the AME Zion Church its whole hearted support and, a few months later, sent a contribution of $4500 for its building fund.

Christmas grave coverings were sold for the first time, all receipts to be credited to the 1959 budget. The canvas was in fair shape as the year closed—about eighty-five percent of the goal had been reached as compared to only seventy-five percent at the same time the previous year.

This was considered very important as many people were moving out of the parish.

At the beginning of 1960, the Churchyard Committee asked that its name be changed to the Cemetery Committee, the canvass was successfully completed and the Scout charter was renewed. All Saints had the unique distinction of sponsoring three Scout units – Cubs, Scouts and Explorers.

The appraiser informed the Vestry that the widening of Middle Neck Road had taken away 10,661 sq. ft. of the church's land for which eleven thousand dollars compensation was offered. At the discussion, several vestrymen pointed out that there had also been injury to the roots of the copper beech tree in front of the church although the tree still appeared to be in good health. Others observed that the church's operating costs had increased because of the 600 ft. of sidewalk and fence which now had to be maintained. Nevertheless, the Vestry voted to accept the sum offered.

Once again the Treasurer had to report that the plate collection for the past year had been lower than the year before. Church School registration was also lower and eight parish families had left Great Neck because they could no longer afford to live in the community.

Changes were made that reflected several trends. In 1960, the Advent communion service for men and boys was opened to women and girls so that it became a family corporate communion. The importance of the work of the women of the parish was mentioned more often at vestry meetings. For the first time, there seemed to be a clear realization that the money brought in by the major women's activities such as the Strawberry Festival and the Thrift Shop was essential to All Saints' financial welfare.

The Curate, James A. Birdall, sent in his formal resignation in January, 1961. He had been at All Saints for almost four years. Mr. McKechnie said that James and Marcia Birdall had given of themselves "unstintingly to the development of the life and work of this parish." Mr. Birdsall recommended that Janet Shepherd take over the youth work. She was a communicant at All Saints, had been a member and officer in the YPF and had taught at the Church School. She was appointed and *The Herald* noted that "she brings to the work a joy of young people and a friendliness that will be a tremendous asset."

The decline in the Church's enrollment caused some anxiety although other annual activities seemed to have remained the same. In an effort to reawaken interest in its work, the Auxiliary Vestry decided to change its name to the All Saints Service Organization. It continued the same activities and did not dissociate itself from the Vestry.

The Day Guild had a particularly active season. The members completed and sent off articles for mission stations in South Dakota and Puerto Rico. Cash was sent also because often more could be obtained by people in the missions buying for themselves than by central purchasing.

A Strawberry Festival

The Strawberry Festival netted about forty three hundred dollars in 1961 despite summer showers. It featured a used jewelry table in addition to its usual attractions—the Busy Needle, Okinawan Table (children's clothes), Used Books, Religious Gift Table, Thrift Shop, Parcel Post table, Gourmet Table, Hot Dog Stand, Homemade Goodies, Apron Table, Country Store, Flower and Plant Mart, Carnival Land, Pony Rides, Makeup Table—Be a Clown, Clam Bar, Luncheon and Dinner. The Festival Committee was very grateful to the Merchant Marine Academy Band for the concert it gave and to the Alert Fire Company for trusting them with one of their engines which was much admired. The Festival Steering Committee suggested that the following year's committee include members from each of the church groups; the Vestry, the Day Guild, St. Margaret's and St. Catherine's. The Vestry accepted the suggestion.

A proposal was made by a vestryman to replace the rectory with a modern home of moderate size and to remove the old parish house which was so expensive to heat. The idea met with great disfavor particularly from the women of the parish and was abandoned.

The Reverend Robert Blakely was appointed the Rector's Assistant and took over the month of September while Mr. McKechnie was in Bermuda. During the summer of 1962, in answer to the request of many parishioners, the summer Sunday service was held at 10 A.M. and it still is.

All Saints Church's 75th Anniversary celebration took place in November. The invited guests included the Rt. Rev. James P. DeWolfe, Bishop of Long Island and two Suffragen Bishops, J.G. Sherman and Charles W. MacLean, the Very Rev. Harold F. Lemoine, Dean of the Cathedral of the Incarnation and the daughters of the Rev. Kirkland Huske, Mrs. Francis Sherrerd and Miss Elsie B. Huske. The Rectors of Christ Church, St. Paul's, Great Neck and all the churches of the Great Neck area were also invited as well as the Rabbis of all the Great Neck Temples and two former Curates, the Rev. Charles E. Baker and the Rev. James A. Birdsall.

On November 11th, 1962, prior to the church service, a new flagpole was dedicated by the Rector honoring the servicemen of the parish and commemorating the 75th anniversary of the consecration of All Saints Church. The cost of the flagpole had been underwritten by the Parish Service Organization, the American flag was a gift of Ralph Fliedner and the Church flag a gift of Mr. and Mrs. Louis Manzino. After the ceremony, the choir led a processional into the church, the people following, all singing "For All the Saints."

The 75th Anniversary program was a four page folder, its cover embossed in gold. It included a list of the invited guests, the parish organization for 1962 and a one page history called "How It Has Happened." The brief history concluded with, ". . . in a very special and a very real way, the worship and work goes on as the life of 'the communion of saints' and we celebrate with deepest and highest joy and thanksgiving the Seventy-fifth Anniversary of All Saints Church here in Great Neck."

In commemoration of the 75th, tiles and plates decorated with a picture of All Saints Church in color were offered for sale at two dollars and fifty cents per plate and one dollar and seventy-five cents per tile. And a fund was started to electrify the chimes. The plan was to be able to operate the chimes electrically so that they could be rung from a small keyboard under the tower stairs and/or from the organ console.

To start the chimes fund, a memorial gift of two hundred dollars was donated through the Book of Memory. The total cost for the electrification of the chimes was estimated at about thirty five hundred dollars, a figure that proved to be unrealistic because the following year an estimate for all the work necessary, including the wiring, was given at seventy five hundred dollars.

At the end of 1962, the Treasurer was happy to announce that the holdings of All Saints Church had increased. However there was some concern over the report that Church School attendance was only one third of what it had been two years earlier. Mr. McKechnie explained that real estate prices and rentals in Great Neck were so high that the young people of the parish were forced to move away.

In February, 1963, the YPF sponsored a program on "The Christian and Loyalty." The speaker was Congressman Stephen Derounian who also presented the parish with an American flag that had flown over the United States Capitol.

A discussion of music in the church was prompted by complaints from some of the parishioners that the familiar hymns which everyone loved were seldom sung during the service. A committee met with Mr. Mc-Edwards, the organist, who agreed to select some of the hymns that the people wanted. He explained that his choices were guided by the seasonal themes of the Episcopal Church. In answer to another request, he promised that the choir would sing more chants.

The death of Wray Landon left a vacancy on the Vestry which Clifford Coddington was elected to fill. A colored burse and a veil was presented to the church in Mr. Landon's memory.

Mr. McKechnie described the pattern of services for the patronal festival, the octave for the Feast of All Saints, that had been developed over the years. Daily communion services were conducted each day during which those members of the parish family who had died since the previous November 1st were remembered by name. At each service, also, some of the names on the Memorial Roll recorded in the Book of Memory were read so that by the end of the octave all the names on the All Saints Memorial Roll had been read.

In February, 1964, the Rector reported on the results of a questionnaire that had been sent to the All Saints parishioners. The statistics revealed that there were fewer children in the Church School than in the past and that the largest number of parishioners were in the fifty to eight-five year old group followed by the forty to fifty year old group with the smallest number in the twenty to thirty-five year old group. Most of the parishioners were home owners who lived within fifteen minutes of the church but did not attend regularly. Plate collections were down from the past year and pledges were about two percent off. The conclusions reached were a disturbing prognosis for the church's future. Great Neck cannot support three Episcopal churches, the report stated. In an attempt to ameliorate the stiuation, Father Norris and three members of the St. Paul's Vestry met with Mr. McKechnie and three members of the All Saints Vestry to plan joint activities. Since the possibility of merger of the two churches seemed remote, the purpose of the plan was to attempt to strengthen both parishes.

Honorary Warden J. Edward Meyer died in September, 1964. His business associates asked that something special in the way of a memorial be given in his honor. With Mrs. Meyer's consent, it was decided to construct a new doorway at the entrance to the church to be known as the J.E. Meyer Memorial Doorway.

On January 11, 1965, the Rector announced his retirement as of September 30, 1965. He reminded everyone that it had been thirty-six years since he had taken over as a summer supply for Mr. Huske, who had died eight days later. Thirty-five years ago this September he had been called to become the Rector of All Saints and it had been a glorious thirty-six years, Mr. McKechnie said, and he hoped that he and his wife had contributed something to the growth and welfare of the parish.

The Vestry was somewhat stunned by the announcement but accepted the resignation and stated for the record that Mr. McKechnie had served faithfully during his ministry at All Saints. "We regret that the McKechnies are leaving but we wish them a happy retirement," the vestrymen added. The Rector agreed to send a letter to the parishioners informing them of his retirement.

A vestry committee was formed to find a new rector and was authorized to spend a reasonable amount of money in the process. The search committee began its work at once. It started out by asking James A. Birdsall, former Curate, to become the Rector of All Saints but he preferred to stay at Grace Church, Broad Brook, Connecticut. The committee members then went to Bishop De Wolfe who gave them the names of eight candidates whom he endorsed. A number of the candidates had accepted other jobs or were eliminated for various reasons until the list was reduced to three. The committee arranged that the three meet with the Vestry before the June vestry meeting. The Rev. Gary E. Maier,

Church of the Advent, Westbury was one of the candidates but, aged twenty-seven, he was considered too young to be a rector. Finally, the committee decided to enlarge its search, promising that when it found the right man it would report first to the vestry then to the parish and then to Bishop De Wolfe.

On July 27, the Vestry called a special meeting for the selection of a new Rector. Earlier, on July 15th, the committee of five vestry members had voted on six candidates with the majority vote going to the Rev. Gary E. Maier. His name was formally presented to the Vestry to be the new rector. Most of the members had met him and two committee members had attended services at his church to hear him preach. Several committee members had visited Mr. Maier at home and met his charming wife. The committee report said that Mr. Maier was a promising young man of twenty-eight who had received his training at General Seminary in New York. He had been recommended enthusiastically by Mr. Underwood, the former Rector of the Church of the Advent, Westbury, with whom he had worked for two years during which he ran the parish's parochial day school. The only problem was that Mr. Maier, presently the Priest-in-Charge at the Westbury church because its Rector, Mr. Underwood, had been transferred to the Cathedral, had agreed to stay in Westbury until December 1st. This difficulty was resolved when Mr. McKechnie agreed to remain as Priest-in-Charge at All Saints until Mr. Maier was free to come to Great Neck.

The Vestry discussed the appointment at great length. Some felt that no appointment should be made until all the vestrymen had heard Mr. Maier preach. Others wanted more time to decide. Finally, a motion was made to approve Mr. Maier's appointment as Rector of All Saints Church starting December 1, 1965. The vote was unanimously in favor of the motion.

Although the selection of a new rector dominated all of the other events of 1965, during the early part of the year, the chimes had been electrified—"Let Our Bells Ring Out / A Joyous Call For Worship."

In May Warden John C. Martin died. "We have lost a good friend and faithful churchman in his untimely death," said the Vestry resolution. Otto Boysen was elected to fill the unfinished term.

The testimonial dinner given for the McKechnies on September 22, 1965 was unprecedented in the numbers present and in its outpouring of respect and affection for the Rector and his wife. Five hundred and thirty people were present including parishioners, friends from other parishes and of other faiths, a large complement of Rabbis and Pastors and Priests and two Long Island Bishops.

James Wells, who was the Mater of Ceremonies, made gracious, full and accurate introductions with just enough wit to keep the occasion from becoming too emotional.

Mr. McKechnie was presented with a plaque from the American Legion for his service in World War I and his work as a founder of the local American Legion Post, a scroll from the Alert Fire Department for his service as Chaplain, a gift certificate from the Lions Club, a scroll from the Rotary Club for his leadership and a scroll from the Board of the Town of North Hempstead acknowledging his constant and active interest in town affairs. Rabbi Jacob Rudin reminisced about his more than thirty year friendship with Mr. McKechnie and their work together in the Great Neck Association of Ministers and Rabbis. Rear Admiral Gordon McLintock, Superintendent of the Kings Point Merchant Marine Academy, mused over the close friendship of the two Scotsmen and how Mr. McKechnie always extended aid to the Academy and its personnel. Robert Ellard, Honorary Warden of All Saints Church and senior parishioner (ninety years old), thanked the McKechnies on behalf of the parish for their inspiring pastoral service.

Warden Clifford Coddington presented a scroll from the Vestry which cited the Rector's faithful and inspiring leadership and designated the Rev. Alexander R. McKechnie as Rector Emeritus of All Saints Church at his official retirement on September 30, 1965. The final presentation was a sixty five hundred dollar purse collected by Mrs. J. Edward Meyer, Chairman of the Honorarium Committee. She said that she hoped that the McKechnies would take a long vacation "perhaps a slow boat to Japan and/or other ports of call."

Mr. Wells then presented the assembled multitude to the Rector so that he could respond to the accolades. He thanked everyone and recalled those in the parish who had helped him, particularly in the early days, such as Mrs. Howard F. Clark, Mrs. John B. Pitman, Mrs. Marks and Mr. Ellard. Then he spoke of his Dorothy and her ever loyal and steadfast help through their eventful years together.

After a long standing ovation for the McKechnies, the blessing was given by Bishop Charles McLean and the dinner was over.

A party was given on October 31st for Elizabeth Frank, the parish secretary for twenty-four years and Hugh McEdwards, the organist and choirmaster for twenty-three years. Both of them were retiring from their positions at All Saints Church.

The Annual Parish Meeting was a memorable one because it witnessed the smooth passing of the torch from one regime to another. Listening to the parting remarks of the Rev. Alexander McKechnie and the introductory remarks of the Rev. Gary Maier, a parishioner wrote, "one could not but think how fortunate we are at All Saints, we can keep our beloved Rector of thirty-five years as Rector Emeritus, while acquiring a new Rector whom we already like very much."

All Saints Church's Altar at Easter during the 1930's

The Rev. Gary E. Maier, the fourth Rector of All Saints Church

4

CHANGE AND A NEW BEGINNING:
The Ministry of Gary E. Maier

The new regime brought with it great energy and some immediate changes. Father Maier appointed Mrs. Harvey Smith the new parish secretary. She was a member of the Church of the Advent, Westbury and well grounded in the ways of Episcopalians. From the start she managed all the demands of her office beautifully.

Mr. and Mrs. Robley Lawson were chosen to be the new choirmaster and organist. They came from a teaching job in Montana but had a notable reputation at such local churches as the Congregational Church, Manhasset. Robley was a voice teacher and Jean, the daughter of a Methodist Minister, also a teacher, had played the organ in church since she was fifteen years old.

Father Maier announced that he would conduct a Healing Service every Wednesday at 10:30 A.M. "Its purpose," he said, "was to bring the helpfulness of religion and faith to bear on fear, anxiety, worry, frustration, guilt, sickness and disease." After Holy Communion and Anointing, there would be a brief study and question period.

Father Maier's Institution took place on February 9, 1966 at 8 P.M. After the procession, which included the choir, the clergy and Bishop Jonathan G. Sherman, Suffragan Bishop of Long Island, entered the church and the processional hymn, "Praise my soul the King of Heaven" was concluded, the Bishop began the Office of Institution. Wardens Otto H.

The Rev. Gary E. Maier installed as the fourth Rector of All Saints Church, December, 1965. With Otto Boysen and Charles Dion, presenting the key.

Boysen and Charles Dion stood at the Altar Rail and presented Father Maier with a large golden key to the Church. Then Bishop Sherman read the Letter of Institution and gave Father Maier a Bible, a Book of Common Prayer and a copy of the books of the canons of the general and diocesan conventions to signify his role as a priest and rector of All Saints Church.

Bishop Sherman's stirring sermon was on "The Continuity of the Church." He pointed out that Father Maier's Institution occurred on the burial day of our Bishop James DeWolfe. He spoke also of the congregation's responsibility to the Church.

A reception for the Maiers in the Parish House followed the service. The E.C.W. had decorated the hall in silver and gold and served punch and cookies. During the reception, the Wardens and Vestry presented Father Maier with a Bible and a Book Of Common Prayer.

The election of a new Bishop took place on March 15, 1966. The All Saints Vestry sent three lay delegates who were instructed to vote for Bishop Sherman unless something unforseen occurred at the Diocesan Convention. Bishop Sherman was elected.

In the spring, the Rector announced that, in conjunction with St. Paul's parish, he would conduct a day camp at All Saints from July 5 to August 12 for about twenty-five children from the ages of five and a half to thirteen. Activities would include religion, arts and crafts, games and swimming. The camp got off to a good start that summer ending up with a small surplus.

All Saints exchange program with Puerto Rico, Fr. Maier and members of the Y.P.F.

Several other young people's projects were started at this time. All Saints parish sent Jeanne Dion and Betsey Imperator to be ambassadors to a Puerto Rican mission church and brought two Puerto Rican students to Great Neck to attend the day camp. A large part of the needed seven hundred and fifty dollars was raised by the young people of the church who held a "Workday for Christ" during which they did odd jobs around the house such as painting the fence, chopping down old trees, cleaning the garage or attic and washing the car or the dog. The balance of the thousand dollars needed was contributed by the Vestry.

The celebration of the Church's 80th Anniversary dominated the 1967 activities. The Rector suggested the publication of a journal that would contain paid advertisements from local merchants, friends and members of All Saints and would appear at the time of the Strawberry Festival. The Committee formed to undertake the task was headed by Barbara Grose and Strahan Davis. The Journal was an immediate success and became an annual fund raising project.

That same year a nursery school was founded at All Saints. Father Maier proposed a small school to start in the fall with about thirty children of all races and religions to be in session five days a week from nine to twelve in the morning. Hopefully, the parents of the nursery school children would help in its organization. The Rector said that good education for three year olds is a duty of the church.

The Vestry accepted the proposal on the condition that the school would be self-sufficient. The school was launched as planned and has continued down the years as a durable part of parish life.

A letter about the 80th Anniversary sent from the Presiding Bishop, John E. Himes, said: "This is indeed an important milestone in the history of your parish and I rejoice with you and your people, praying for you God's richest blessing upon the continued growth of your work and witness in His name." Bishop Sherman of Long Island wrote a particularly memorable letter on the occasion of the 80th. "All Saints Church is part of the great stream of divine life flowing down through the ages of man . . ." he said. "We tend to think of the Saints as those who are commemorated in stained glass or on days marked on the Christian calendar. But the New Testament teaches us that by virtue of Holy Baptism we are all saints. Throughout Christian history, the work of the saints has been to bring all the varied interests and activities of mankind into an ordered relationship under the sovereignty of Christ. It is because All Saints Church has continued steadfastly in this purpose that we rejoice and give thanks on this eightieth anniversary."

On November 5 at 4 P.M., the adult choir augmented by friends, under the direction of Robley Lawson, presented a musical tribute to the 80th Anniversary. Two great masterworks were offered; J.S. Bach's "The Lord is a Sun and Shield," composed for Reformation Sunday, 1737 and Anton Bruckner's "Te Deum." Jean Lawson played the refurbished organ.

In 1967, an important liturgical change was introduced at the 9:30 service. On the first Sunday of the month, when the offering was presented, an usher brought up the bread and wine, which had been placed on the small Altar at the back of the church, for consecration at the Altar. Gradually, this change was adopted at all services.

At the 1967 Annual Meeting, which took place on December 4th after a covered dish supper served by the women of the Church, some important new matters were discussed. The Rector reported that the newly founded nursery school was now certified as one of the Diocesan parochial schools. He then acquainted the parish with an innovative plan for handling church finances. This entailed turning over to the Vestry all the profits from the Strawberry Festival and other fund raising projects to be used for the building restoration fund. The womens groups, which were those most affected by this plan, were amenable to the new financial arrangements. They voted to turn over their Strawberry Festival rainy day account of seven thousand dollars as well as all future Strawberry Festival money and other proceeds with the exception of five hundred dollars which would be used as seed money for the Festival and be included in the annual budget for E.C.W. work.

At Father Maier's request, the Day Guild agreed to turn over the Thrift Shop proceeds and the greater part of their savings account which altogether amounted to a sum of at least twelve thousand dollars.

The major issue, however, was the news that the Episcopal Church now permitted women to serve on vestries. The admission of women to the All Saints vestry required a change in the charter, Father Maier explained. This meant that the admission of women had to be approved by the Vestry and then brought to the next Annual Parish Meeting or to a special parish meeting for a vote. After discussion, the majority of those present endorsed the admission of women to the Vestry if the Vestry approved of the change.

At its December meeting, as directed, the Vestry took up the question of admission of women to the Vestry. After discussion, Mr. Bartlett moved that "It is the sense of this meeting that the Wardens and Vestrymen believe that women should be permitted to serve on the Vestry of All Saints Church, and such legal steps as are necessary be taken to grant this permission." There was an affirmative vote with one abstention.

The first Sunday after Epiphany was appointed to be the first Sunday at which the trial liturgy, which had been prepared by the Standing Liturgical Commission of the Episcopal Church, was to be used. At All Saints, after ample study, the congregation "got its feet wet with this new and beautiful service of Holy Communion. Our hats go off to the ushers, choir, acolytes and all the congregation who followed and participated with noble precision," *The Herald* reported.

The new liturgy was to be used for a trial period of about six months, after which time, the parishioners were to be asked to give constructive criticism of it. The information obtained was to be forwarded in writing to the Standing Liturgical Commission.

During the six months trial period, Father Maier followed the Bishop's directive to use the proposed liturgy to its fullest advantage by utilizing its flexibility as to structure, rubric, use of music and length of service. During Lent, the Rector celebrated the trial liturgy at the Tuesday night Lenten meetings. After the service, there was instruction and discussion at the Rectory.

Some gifts were received at this time. Mr. Bartlett gave shares of stock which the Vestry decided to put aside for a fund to be used to hire a Curate. Mr. Roesler contributed a generous sum for the restoration of the cloisters. Henry Harvey relettered Bishop Littlejohn's headstone.

The tragic death of Martin Luther King inspired Father Maier's

Bishop Littlejohn's headstone relettered, May 1967 by our resident stone mason, Mr. Henry Harvey

statements from the pulpit on Palm Sunday regarding the need for creating a better understanding between all races in the cause of Christian brotherhood in the parish. The Vestry went on record in wholehearted support of the Rector's statements.

The 1966 Strawberry Festival was dedicated to Robert A. Ellard who was born in 1869. He is "a stalwart parishioner of All Saints Church who sat on the ground as a boy and watched the church being built. He dedicated a great deal of his life to the church as vestryman and warden. We praise God for his service and his brilliant historical writing of Great Neck and especially of All Saints Church," *The Journal* said.

Samuel Walker, who was ordained to the Diaconate in June, became the new curate. He helped the Rector with parish calls and other parochial duties but his work was primarily with the young people. With his assistance, the summer day camp reported a successful season with an enrollment of about forty children. The Nursery School was also doing well with twenty-eight children signed up for the coming year. Mrs. Walker, the new curate's wife, was one of the professional teachers.

The question of women's role in the church was in the forefront at this time. Since the women's groups were turning over their profits to the Vestry instead of managing the money themselves, they were invited to the November Vestry Meeting to discuss their budget and to ask questions on the work of the vestry.

At the Annual Parish Meeting the question of women on the Vestry was settled with a resolution. It read: "Resolved that the qualifications of Wardens and Vestrymen of this Parish shall be that such Wardens and Vestrymen shall be elected only from male and female persons qualified to vote at any annual election or special meeting." The resolution, adopted by secret ballot, with forty-one voting yes and thirty-two voting no, was attached to the All Saints Church Charter. Thus, beginning in December, 1969, women were eligible to serve on the vestry.

The year, 1969, began with some financial difficulties. Expenditures in '68 had exceeded those of the previous year by more than twenty thousand dollars, a situation that was characterized by one Vestryman as "awesome." The increase in costs was attributed to higher salaries for the paid singers, pension premiums, and buildings and grounds, cemetery and canvass expenses. The problem was further complicated by the need for many more repairs such as new roofing, replacement and repair of rotted wood, painting of the exterior of the buildings and repair of the organ. A conservative estimate of the cost was one hundred thousand dollars. Father Maier appointed a Long Range Planning Committee to deal with the crisis. Its goal was the reconstruction of the All Saints buildings. Peter Paul Muller, a well known architect, was engaged to go over the buildings, prepare plans and set priorities.

The Vestry then decided to bring these financial problems to the attention of the members of All Saints Church. Many of the parishioners, some Vestrymen felt, were under the impression that the church had so enormous an endowment that money was always plentiful.

Mr. Muller inspected the buildings and came up with a report that divided the necessary work into two categories. First, he recommended a general restoration of the physical plant and then, second, consideration of alterations and possible additions. As to priorities, Mr. Muller suggested that the work begin with the removal of all exterior wood and its replacement with new wood in a natural color. Next, he said, new sills should be installed in the windows of Huske Hall. The Rector said that he would study the recommendations.

At this time, the parish was proud to learn that Father Maier had been elected to the Board of Managers of the Church Charity Foundation of Long Island which administers St. John's Hospital in Brooklyn and Smithtown. He followed in the footsteps of Mr. McKechnie who had served on the board and had been instrumental in the successful completion of the new St. John's Hospital, Smithtown.

For its 1969 Lenten program, All Saints undertook support of St. Barnabas' Episcopal Church in Brooklyn which had just opened its doors to a predominantly West Indian congregation. The program included the donation of All Saints' Lenten offerings to the new church and participation in an exchange program. The All Saints secondary school students went to St. Barnabas to worship, study and socialize and Father John Taylor of St. Barnabas and Father Maier exchanged pulpits.

The chronic question of the merging of All Saints' and St. Paul's vestries came up again at this time because of Father Norris' resignation from St. Paul's. A committee from All Saints met with a committee from St. Paul's but, although the Bishop was said to favor the merger and a precedent had been set by the mergers of some churches in Brooklyn, the St. Paul's committee did not give its unanimous support.

Robert A. Ellard, dedicated churchman and historian of All Saints

On Sunday, November 2nd, the one hundredth birthday of Robert A. Ellard was celebrated. Holy Communion was offered to the glory of God in thanksgiving for Mr. Ellard's long and faithful life of service. Tributes were read from President Nixon, the Bishop of Long Island, the Lions Club, the Rotary Club and the Mayor of the Village of Great Neck who proclaimed November 2, 1969, Robert A. Ellard Day. Following the service, there was a reception with a huge birthday cake and the reading of more tributes including a proclamation from the Supervisor of the Town of North Hempstead declaring Nov. 2nd Robert A. Ellard day in the Town.

In preparation for the 1969 Annual meeting, two important resolutions were passed by the Vestry. The first one declared women qualified to serve on the Vestry, the second adopted a plan for a rotating vestry. A warden, after serving three consecutive two year terms would not be eligible for reelection for a year and a vestryman who served two consecutive three year terms would not be eligible for reelection for a year.

The Vestry was very much concerned by the architect's report which revealed many unsuspected problems. Mr. Muller had visited the site and decided that some areas required immediate work while others could wait for a later date. However, he said, it would be necessary to draw plans for all of the buildings because either the original specifications could not be found or they were inadequate. After one building was done, he added, he could give more exact estimates.

The Vestry discussed the Muller Report and decided that the buildings must be restored before they fell apart. They also engaged Peter Paul Muller to prepare the plans as outlined at a cost not to exceed five thousand dollars and to be completed by April 15, 1970.

When the architect's drawings arrived, the Vestrymen studied them carefully. They decided that repairs to the exteriors of the church and parish house be done first and then the interiors of the buildings. They also agreed to accept Mr. Muller's suggestion to employ Clyde M. Alston to do the mechanical work.

John Lawrence was appointed curate in 1970. He was a resident of Valley Stream and a graduate of General Theological Seminary who was ordained to the diaconate on June 13th. He offered a great deal of experience and success in community action and in working with young people. After a search for the right house for Mr. Lawrence and his family, the Vestry approved the purchase of 1 Appletree Lane.

The Rev. Alexander McKechnie, Rector Emeritus of All Saints Church, died on May 13, 1970. Bishop MacLean was the celebrant at the funeral service which took place at All Saints Church and Hugh McEdwards was the organist. "For thirty-seven years he served our Parish as its Rector," the memorial resolution read. "He served his God, country, community, the missionary field, the Diocesan Church and this Parish with great and special gifts."

All Saints was greatly honored when its warden, James Wells, was elected to the Diocesan council, an advisory body to the Bishop, at the 107th Annual Convention. He gave a brilliant presentation emphasizing the importance of the traditional values of the Episcopal Church within the Anglican Communion.

The new liturgy, which was being used the third Sunday of each month at the 10:30 Service, was being resisted by many parishioners. The Vestry discussed its own reservations about it and its concern that the new liturgy did not have the support of the church members. The clergy should be responsive to the people, it said. The Rector replied by informing the Vestry that the General Convention of the Episcopal Church held in October, 1970, had approved the trial use of the revised liturgy.

Any further delay in dealing with the renovations for the old parish house and Huske Hall became impossible because the buildings failed to meet fire regulations. A vestry committee that met with the Rector and Mr. Muller concluded that the best plan was to concentrate on the Church and Huske Hall beginning with satisfying the fire regulations and then undertaking a complete renovation of the kitchen and the church tower.

There were quite a number of vacant vestry seats at the 1970 Annual Meeting as many of the vestrymen were ineligible for reelection. Among those elected was Anne Rowland, All Saints' first vestrywoman. Her election put All Saints in step with the National Church which had seated women delegates for the first time in the history of the Anglican Church at its 1970 meeting.

The annual financial report was disappointing. Insurance and other costs were up whereas the plate collection and pledge income had declined from the past year. The stock market was down which had reduced the value of the church holdings. One Vestryman warned the parishioners that capital funds were being drawn on. Another advised that some new ways of raising money must be devised.

Mr. Muller attended the December Vestry meeting to report on the restoration program. He presented photographs that showed the deterioration of the church tower's wood which was so advanced that the chimes, which were set in steel casing, were keeping the tower in place. After the architect left, Father Maier said that the time had come for the Vestry to work on a serious fund raising campaign. The only available money for the repairs was the Roesler fund which was earmarked for the restoration of the cloisters.

The restoration fund received a needed boost when private individuals pledged twenty-six hundred dollars to restore the clock tower. It was decided then that the next areas to be attended to would be the west facade of the church and the Meyer Memorial entrance.

Father Lawrence was progressing enthusiastically and successfully with his plan for youth work. His first effort was the improvement of the curriculum of the church school by using an effective new series for teachers called "A Journey in Faith." The Curate founded an Acolytes Guild, with Juniors and Seniors in the same group, that had as one of its activities Saturday morning Communion breakfasts and instruction. He also introduced such new activities for the E.Y.C as dances, bake sales and retreats.

The Vestry was very sorry to learn that Father Lawrence was leaving All Saints to accept a position as Assistant Rector at Grace Church, Nyack, New York, effective on October 1st. With the high cost of the restoration and the loss of more families who had moved away, the Vestry considered doing without a curate but Father Maier pointed out that assistance was imperative to continue the work with the young people. A compromise was reached with the decision to sell the Appletree Lane house which Father Lawrence had occupied and to hire a new curate.

A new directive from the Diocesan Convention, which was announced at the 1971 Annual Parish Meeting, stated that eighteen year olds were now eligible to vote at parish meetings and to run for the vestry. And, at the same meeting, the Treasurer reported with pleasure that the twelve thousand dollar deficit had been reduced to two thousand dollars.

At the beginning of 1972, a new Book of Memory was started because the old one had been filled. At the Rector's suggestion, the new book was dedicated to Robert A. Ellard.

In an article published in *The Herald*, Father Maier discussed the progress of the new liturgy. Bishop Sherman, he said, had directed that Rite 2 in the "Services for Trial Use" be used starting with Whitsunday. However, All Saints will use Rite 1 for a period of time at the 10:30 Service. "Please share your feelings with me so that we may be responsible members of the Episcopal Church as it adopts its ancient worship to the present," Father Maier wrote. In order to carry out the Diocesan directive, the Rector ordered two hundred copies of the green book containing the trial liturgies to be placed in the pews. He promisd to preach sermons on the new liturgy in order to explain the changes and additions to the congregation.

Some parishioners were honored at this time. A Vestry resolution honored Henry W. Harvey for his devoted work. The Distinguished Service Cross was presented to Jesse Erickson in recognition of fifty-four

Church Tower rebuilt and refurbished

years of service on the Altar Guild. For thirty-five years, she had cared for the choir vestments and supervised the distribution of the Altar flowers to the sick.

Work on the church restoration progressed. The tower, which had been destroyed by dry rot and termites, was completely rebuilt. The clock was refaced and set. The porte-cochere and the Meyer memorial were returned to their original beauty. The Church, which in its original state had been plain wood and then, at a later time, painted a dismal black, was restored to a color as close to the original as possible. The chimney was rebuilt and the roof refinished. All of Huske Hall was rewired.

The total cost of the restoration was now estimated at approximately two hundred and fifty thousand dollars of which one hundred and six thousand dollars had been spent already. Father Maier said that the summary of the cost was a challenge to the parishioners to contribute more. "We wish to maintain this beautiful Church in perfect order for it is, in fact, the house of God. The home where so many have worshipped in the past and where so many will worship in the future."

Always aware of and involved in community activities, All Saints Church honored the Golden Jubilee of the Village of Great Neck, June, 1972 with an old fashioned Hymn sing at its 10:30 Service. The parishioners chose their favorites which were played by Jean Lawson and sung by all with great enthusiasm.

The Every Member Canvass for 1972, which was headed by Frank Glover and Anne Rowland, was memorable because, for the first time, women as well as men were canvassers.

Two controversial issues, as yet unresolved, were brought up at the Annual Parish Meeting. The first one concerned the installation of an Ambry on the Altar for storing the Blessed Sacrament which was and still is kept in the Sacristy in marked cruets. The Vestry had turned down the suggestion three times in the past on the grounds that the use of an Ambry was too similar to the rites of the Roman Catholic Church. The Rector favored the Ambry because keeping the Sacrament in the Sacristy closet, the Altar Guild reported, had led to errors in keeping the consecrated wine separate. An open discussion resulted in a motion that was passed which requested Father Maier to send a questionnaire to the parishioners to determine their opinions on the subject.

The second matter was a proposal to reduce the number of vestrymembers by not filling the vacancies as they came up. The Rector explained that the number of vestry members had been increased to fifteen when the chapel had to be taken care of. After St. Paul's was established as a parish, the number of All Saints vestrymembers had remained the same. According to canon law, in order to change the number, the request must go before an Annual Meeting. The Vestry had not acted on the suggestion because it agreed with the Rector that a large vestry was an advantage since there were times when some members could not attend meetings. The Annual Meeting did not take any action on the proposal.

When the subject of a merger between All Saints and St. Paul's was reintroduced at a Vestry meeting, Rudy Kopf offered to hold a dinner for the vestrymembers of both churches. St. Paul's Vestry refused the invitation but did agree to joint informal talks, possibly about music programs, in the hope of alleviating the tension between the two Great Neck Episcopal Churches. Nothing came of the idea. On the contrary, matters were not improved because at regional meetings with other parishes for the purpose of cooperation in programs and plans, All Saints met with Nassau churches and St. Paul's chose to meet with churches in Flushing and Queens.

During this period, Father David Keller, who was finishing his studies for a doctorate, was the Assistant Minister. Under the direction of the Kellers, the All Saints-St Paul's Day Camp offered a special Arts and Crafts program centered on Indian and Alaskan artifacts. Father Keller had lived in Alaska for eleven years and was returning there to become the Director of Christian Education. Upon leaving Great Neck in June, Father Keller said he and his family had thoroughly enjoyed being at All Saints and appreciated the warmth and welcome they had received.

In February, 1974, All Saints parish was proud to learn that Father Maier had been elected to the College of Preachers and would be at the National Cathedral in Washington in March. This was a great honor as only twenty clergymen from all over the world were invited to attend the college annually.

The tremendous expenditure that had been made for the Church's rehabilitation occupied much of the discussion at Vestry meetings. Among the suggestions offered was the proposal to establish a capital fund for future major repairs since all agreed that the endowment fund could not stand another such major invasion of its resources. The finance committee was encouraged to forge ahead with its maintenance fund drive. The hope was that the parish would contribute fifteen thousand dollars which the Vestry would match. The five thousand dollar profit from the Strawberry Festival and the Journal was given to the fund and about twenty-five hundred dollars collected from the parish but this was not enough to relieve the financial pinch. The Rector decided to dispense with the services of an Assistant to help the Church's financial crisis. And, by the end of the year, the maintenance fund did reach ten thousand dollars.

A special diocesan session was called for November 16, 1974 to elect a Bishop Coadjutor to succeed Bishop Sherman. All Saints Church sent Brock Lownes and Paul C. White, Jr. as lay delegates with Clifton Hicks and J. Charles Frank, Jr. as alternates. At the session, Robert C. Witcher, Rector of the Episcopal Church in Baton Rouge, Louisiana, was elected. Father Maier and delegates Lownes and Frank had voted for him.

At the Annual Parish Meeting, Henry W. Harvey was elected Warden and Ethel Marks was the third woman elected to the Vestry after Anne Rowland and Grace Miller, now Clerk of the Vestry. The end of the year financial report was more encouraging than had been anticipated. The pledges for 1975 were expected to exceed the estimate and the Treasurer reported that the surplus would be equal or better than the previous year.

A living creche - before the animals took off down Middle Neck Road

The '74 Christmas programs were highly successful and innovative. A live creche in front of the Church was received with great popular interest and some amusement when one or two of the animals escaped down Middle Neck Road with the Rector and others in full pursuit. The presentation of "The Messiah" drew the largest audience that had ever attended a church performance. It only split even financially but great joy was given to hundreds of people.

Money matters dominated the work of the Vestry at the start of 1975. Although All Saints was getting along better than many of the churches in the diocese, eleven of which had to close, there were problems. A survey revealed that more than fifty percent of the pledges came from retired parishioners who lived on fixed incomes. After much discussion along familiar lines of cutting back on the cost of the music, it was decided to try to search out small economies. Such measures as eight Sundays without paid singers, elimination of the cost of a choir vestment allowance and of a paid secretary to take the minutes were introduced. Efforts to lower the deficit were and are chronic concerns at most churches.

At the 1975 Annual Meeting, Gerald Roberts was elected Warden. Father Maier pointed out that All Saints Church, which was beginning its ninetieth year, was a diaspora church from which many had gone out to preach – over twenty priests. He thanked the parish for the party that it had given him to celebrate his tenth anniversary as their Rector.

In 1976, the Church acquired a Sunday assistant, the Rev. Wiley Merryman, an older man with a great deal of experience who taught a Sunday Bible class.

At the '76 Annual Parish Meeting, discussion was initiated again on the question of the size of the Vestry. The proposal was made to reduce the Vestry from fifteen members to seven to ten members plus two Wardens because the population of the parish was much reduced. Debate was heated. Those opposed to the reduction emphasized that a large Vestry involved many in church work. The meeting accepted that reasoning and defeated the proposal.

In January, Rudy Kopf gave All Saints seventeen thousand dollars for the renovation of the stained glass windows and the installation of protective covering for them. This was received with gratitude because the fear of vandalism destroying the precious glass had been a great source of worry.

Father Maier presented the revised Book of Common Prayer to the Vestry at its February meeting. He pointed out that it had been worked on for many years and was the first one in history to have input from the people who would use it in their worship. Bishop Sherman had provided guidance for reading the new prayer book and All Saints' St. Catherine's Guild had purchased copies for the congregation. This introduction was only the beginning of discussions and of reservations expressed by the members of the Vestry and others on the sensitive subject of the new Book of Common Prayer.

In April, the new prayer books were placed in the pews. Earlier, Father Maier had asked the vestrymembers to take copies home to read. "Let us not judge until we have read and learned it," he cautioned. The first dissent came from a vestrymember who observed that churches were dropping out of the Episcopal Church because of the new prayer book and, he added, the ordination of women. The latter issue was also of great interest to All Saints because Barbara Kelley, a parishioner, was attending General Seminary with the support of the parish.

The Church, at this time, received some welcome funds from the estate of Madeline Dyson and from the sale of a piece of property it owned called Casa Blanca. The Vestry also decided to take the management of its endowment funds out of the hands of Citibank and to give it, for the trial period of a year, to Sterling, Grace & Co. who offered the service gratis and charged only fifty percent of the trading commission, which would save the Church a sizeable sum.

Bishop Witcher was installed on June 25, 1977 at 9:30 A.M. at the Cathedral of the Incarnation in Garden City. All Saints Church was represented at the impressive ceremony by Father Maier and Wardens Henry Harvey and Gerald Roberts.

The magnificent and symbolic copper beech tree that stood in front of the Church was found to be suffering from fungus disease and from root cutting that had occurred when Middle Neck Road had been widened. The tree was treated but it continued to fail and the Rector asked for the parishioners' prayers for the noble tree.

At the 1977 Annual Parish Meeting, special tribute was paid to the E.C.W. upon whose dedicated work at the Strawberry Festivals and Christmas Bazaars the Church depended so heavily. The Rector spoke especially of Kitty Poons who had met him and his family at the door of the Rectory on their first day in Great Neck to help them and ever since had been totally dedicated to All Saints working in the Sunday School and many other activities. A special medal was presented to her.

Father Maier also singled out for praise the Church's two seminarians, Geoffrey Imperator, now a Navy Chaplain, and Barbara Kelley, a Junior at General Seminary.

James Wells, Sr. spoke about Rudolph C. Kopf's special work for All

Saints Church and presented him with a plaque. At the presentation, the recipient received a standing ovation.

Father Maier then introduced the sensitive subject of the new Book of Common Prayer with the assurance that he had read every word of it. He explained some of the changes and additions such as the substitution of a "Thanksgiving for Childbirth" for the old "Churching of Women." Though there was still a three year period before the book would be permanently accepted, the Bishop had advised the clergy to use it.

The parishioners answered the Rector with some of their objections to the new prayer book. "The words are awkward," one person said. The book "saps the guts out of five hundred years of tradition; it's splitting parishes and dioceses; there are too many options;" were other dissenting remarks. The Rector answered the objections by citing some of the mistakes that had been corrected as, for example, in the filioque. But, despite his eloquent defense, many were not ready to accept the new book because the familiarity and tradition of the old one was very dear to them.

In 1978, All Saints Church considered applying for landmark status for several of the buildings. There was correspondence and several meetings with the commission but, after careful consideration, the Vestry decided that the disadvantages, such as a loss of some control over the facades of the buildings, outweighed the advantages and so tabled the matter.

The constant and highly charged question of the merger, or reunion, as one vestryperson phrased it, of All Saints and St. Paul's was discussed again with the serious hope that the rejoining of the two parishes would take place. Bishop Witcher met with the All Saints Vestry in June, 1978. Warden Henry Harvey welcomed "Robert, our Bishop," and said that he believed that a united Episcopal Church in Great Neck would create a greater and stronger Christian witness in a predominantly Jewish town as Jesus created a Christian witness in Jerusalem.

The Bishop answered that he had met the year before with the St. Paul's vestry and had requested a profile of their parish. He found that the members of St. Paul's Vestry had strong reservations about reunion, a resistance that had historical roots. Bishop Witcher believed that the merger could occur but, he pointed out, church animosities die hard and people have long memories. A Bishop can encourage a parish reunion but not require it, Bishop Witcher added. He then recommended that the All Saints profile be updated and cautioned against the spreading of rumors which would surely end the chance of reunion. Such a merger, the Bishop concluded would not be "Big Brother" taking over but rather the union of equals.

Many parishioners requested that the 1978 Annual Meeting be held in the daytime on Sunday instead of on Advent Monday. The Vestry agreed to change the Annual Parish meeting to the first Sunday in December and to have it preceded by a covered dish luncheon.

At the meeting, Henry Harvey was reelected Warden with the election of five Vestrymembers. J. Charles Frank, Jr. was elected Treasurer.

The hope expressed at the Annual Meeting that a merger between All Saints and St. Paul's would take place in the near future was destroyed by a letter received from Bishop Witcher in February, 1979. He is "frustrated," he wrote. "I have discussed this matter with both the Rector and Vestry of St. Paul's and there seems to be no desire to move in this direction. . . Under the present circumstances, I do not see any possibility of a merger. I think to press it would cause it only to be a little further down the road."

Father Maier reported in October that he and all the clergy on Long Island had received a letter from Bishop C.S. Mallory, the Assistant Bishop of Long Island, on "Spiritual Renewal." The Rector was pleased to note that All Saints was doing already some of the recommended activities such as offering a Healing Service and a Prayer Group.

The 1979 Annual meeting and covered dish luncheon took place as voted upon on Sunday, December 2 at noon. Gerald Roberts was elected warden along with four vestrymembers. A white pall given in memory of Ford Bartlett was dedicated at the morning service. Episocopal Distinguished Service Crosses were presented to Dorothy McKechnie, Grace Miller, Louis Manzino and Mimi Frank.

At the December Vestry meeting, Father Maier introduced the Ven. Canon William Penny, former Archdeacon of Long Island to discuss the preparation of a parish profile. It had been requested by the Bishop "to evaluate with the head as well as the heart" the need for merging the Great Neck Episcopal Churches.

Vestrymembers were intimidated by the amount of work involved in getting out a parish profile but Father Penny promised to guide the committee step by step. The first step would be a meeting of parish members, spearheaded by the Vestry, to assemble data according to formulae worked out by Father Penny. Then Father Penny would conduct a six hour workshop to organize the submitted data.

The actual method used to achieve the desired result was then revealed. Groups of people would work together in twenty, thirty and sixty minute time slots discussing, brainstorming, establishing priority goals, deciding what was vital, important or just nice until a concise statement of practical aims emerged. The hard data which resulted from the surveys would then be recorded without editorialising. What was most important, Father Penny emphasized, was that the true feelings of the parishioners were expressed.

The Parish Profile was prepared by a staff of thirty parishioners. It was coordinated by the Rector, Wardens Henry Harvey and Gerald Roberts, Vestryman James Rogers and the Chairman, J. Charles Frank, Jr. The Parish Profile Editor and Production Director was Kathleen Vilander. Father Maier wrote that much value would result from the preparation and study of the conclusions of the Profile, 'in that we will have a clearer view, both with the head and the heart, of ourselves, our service to our people, and our relationship with our community, our Church and our God.' The contents of the Profile included a description of the physical setting of All Saints Church, a population study, a family questionnaire, a description of the church's physical plant, and a brief historical sketch of the Church and the Churchyard. A statistical breakdown of Church membership and a report on Christian Education both Sunday School and Confirmation followed.

Part Two of the Profile listed and described the duties and functions of the parish organizations, the vestry and the lay service. The non-religious use of the buildings section stated that "much community service is extended" through the non-religious use of buildings in the All Saints complex. The Rector and the Vestry regard it also "as an extension of Christian witness in a predominantly Jewish area." Alcoholics Anonymous and Overeaters Anonymous were cited as examples of service organizations that used the buildings.

Data on finances and stewardship concluded the researched sections of the pamphlet.

The conclusions reached were many and varied. Among them were the expectations of the clergy and the laity. The clergy's first and highest expectation was "for spirituality, linked closely with a loving, caring joy of religion. Compassion, humor, leadership and reinforcement come to mind as vital to the functions of good priesthood."

The laity wanted to "do our utmost to live up to, in our daily lives, the literal words of Jesus Christ—join together in worship at church and in prayer. . . in fact, love God and our neighbors as ourselves."

The survey revealed that the number one goal for the parishioners of All Saints was "the value of unifying and strengthening the Christian religious community in Great Neck, preferably by the rejoining of the two Episcopal parishes in one, thus increasing membership, financial stability and lessening the drain of maintenance of two large church complexes." Other vital goals were the creation and strengthening of youth groups, preferably with the help of a curate, a creative approach to stewardship and the continued repair and maintenance of All Saints buildings. Among the "nice to do" goals was, first and foremost, "To see the CHURCH FULL!"

The first copy of the Parish Profile was presented to Bishop Witcher who was told that it was done by the All Saints congregation, as requested, "with head and heart."

A letter from Rudolph Kopf was received by the Vestry congratulating those involved in the preparation of the Parish Profile for their fine work and enclosing a check to cover its cost.

A highlight of the winter of 1980 was the presentation of "Godspell" by the young people of the Church and friends. Its three performances attracted an audience of four hundred and earned a small profit. But its importance to the parish went well beyond that because it reflected the enthusiasm of the youngsters involved and promoted community spirit. The performance of "Godspell" at the 10:30 A.M. Sunday service was particularly effective. To the surprise of many, some of the old-line parishioners were pleased when Communion was served during the performance.

Barbara Kelley was ordained a deacon at the Cathedral of the Incarnation, Garden City in April. Many All Saints parishioners attended the ordination and the reception in Huske Hall that followed. Deacon Kelley was engaged to serve as curate at All Saints three days a week. Her ministry included such pastoral services as visiting the sick and shut-ins, confirmation classes and Bible classes.

The question of a merger of All Saints and St. Paul's revived when the Vestry heard that a merger between St. Paul's and St. Philip and St. James, Lake Success had been denied by the Bishop. Father Maier restated his position that Christian witness from one strong Episcopal church was needed in this community. However, the impetus must come from the church itself and St. Paul's was not ready to give up. A church cannot just disband and sell, the Rector explained. The Diocesan Standing Committee has the final word on all property and assets. The Bishop was seeking a formula for the Great Neck situation. And so the matter stands at this writing.

At the annual elections, Henry Harvey, no longer eligible for reelection as warden, was elected Honorary Warden for life. George Bullen was elected Warden along with three Vestrypersons. Father Maier dedicated the 1980 Annual Meeting, which was attended by sixty-eight parishioners, to Warden Henry Harvey and to Dorothy McKechnie whose 85th birthday was on that day. In his comments on the year's work, the Rector said that the Vestry continued efforts to proclaim the Gospel in the community and to maintain the buildings that house our center of worship. Copies of the completed All Saints Church, Great Neck Parish Profile 1980 were circulated to all parishioners.

The Rev. Barbara Kelley, who had been elected to the curacy at Kennet Square, Pennsylvania, took leave of the All Saints Vestry at their February meeting. She thanked the Vestry for their six year support of her through to her ordination. The Vestry's ministration to her, she said, enabled her to minister to the congregation. She said, also, that the Bishop of Pennsylvania was urging her speedy ordination to the priesthood. The Vestry, in its turn, passed a resolution in honor of the Rev. Barbara Kelley, "our good friend and lifelong parishioner." It wished her "Godspeed in her new Parish."

In order to protect the church's many valuable, unique and irreplaceable treasures such as the bells, the organs, the rood screen, the Altar silver etc., it was decided to photograph them and to have new appraisals made for insurance purposes. The project was completed and the cost generously underwritten.

When it became known that St. Paul's property was down-zoned, an attempt was made to meet with the leadership of St. Paul's. But it became clear, once again, that the membership of St. Paul's wished to keep their independence. However, the traditional All Saints 1982 dinner dance was held as a joint celebration with St. Paul's to demonstrate a basic spirit of friendship between the two Great Neck Episcopal Churches.

At the Annual Parish Meeting, the proposed slate, J. Charles Frank, Jr. for warden, and six vestrymembers, was elected unanimously. Gerald Roberts was elected lifetime Honorary Warden and presented with a cross that had been worn by the late Robert A. Ellard hereafter to be known as the Robert A. Ellard award. Warden Roberts responded with deep feeling, moved to tears by "the undreamed of honor." He said, further, that he had been happy and privileged to serve All Saints.

Father Maier announced that Barbara Kelley was to be ordained to the priesthood in mid-December and that he planned to attend the ordination. It had been her idea to hold a Matthew 25 auction which had brought in over a thousand dollars in bids for donated items. Gerald Houck, now a lay reader and Chalice administrator, was the auctioneer.

The new 1982 Vestry elected J. Charles Frank, Jr. Treasurer and LaVerne Goldberg Clerk of the Vestry at its January meeting. Bishop Witcher visited All Saints Church for Confirmation on February 28th. In a solemn and inspiring Service, both children and adults were confirmed. A reception followed.

In April, the parish was saddened to hear that Robley and Jean Lawson were going to retire to Florida. A search committee was formed to find an organist, and, in September, decided to hire Charles Pramnieks, a Julliard student whom Jean Lawson recommended highly.

All Saints Church honors Rabbi Jacob Rudin of Temple Beth-El, Great Neck

The death of Rabbi Jacob Rudin of Temple Beth-El, Great Neck was reported to the All Saints parishioners by Father Maier. All Saints bell tolled eighty times to mark his passing.

At the Annual Parish Meeting, George H. Bullen was elected Warden along with three new Vestrymembers. The Rector commented that All Saints Church was among the first to welcome women to the Vestry. Honorary Warden Gerald Roberts talked to the meeting about the duties and responsibilities of Vestry members. When monies come in, the Vestry controls the funds, he said. It is these funds that keep the church and cemetery complex operating. Therefore, serious dedication is required of the new Vestrymembers.

The Rector's Service Cross was presented to Morgan Grace by Warden Frank. The citation said that Mr. Grace is "a man whose financial genius made our survival possible." He rebuilt our financial standing after our great outlay of endowment capital for the restoration of our buildings. The Rector's Service Cross was presented, also, to Arthur Kelley for his many years of dedication to the needs of All Saints.

1982 marked the twentieth anniversary of Father Maier's ordination to the ministry. To celebrate the important occasion, the All Saints parishioners hosted a reception in their Rector's honor. He and Mrs. Maier were presented with a check to finance a trip to the Holy Land which, they said, they planned for early 1983.

The Holy Land expediton was a source of great joy and inspiration for the Maiers. On the Sunday of their return from their travels, the Rector delivered a stirring sermon on the experience saying that he was moved beyond words to stand where Jesus stood. The sermon, filled with personal recollections of people whom the Maiers met and places they had visited, concluded with some memorable statements about Jerusalem. Father Maier said: "A city filled with unbelievable poverty and great affluence. A city, home to three great religions of the world. A city, filled with snow and rain, sleet and cold, but only twenty miles away is the hot desert on the Jordan plain. It is our city—yours and mine—for all Christians see Jerusalem as their spiritual home."

"The symbol of All Saints Church, Great Neck, is the Jerusalem Cross, also known as the Crusaders' Cross, for we are the crusaders for Jesus Christ of this generation. The spiritual Jerusalem we crave is a walled city fortress, walled against hatred, prejudice, sin and every kind of oppression of man and woman. A City of Hope, an Eternal City."

At the coffee hour that followed the Service, Father Maier showed slides of the places he and Mrs. Maier visited while in the Holy Land.

A pair of wrought-iron chancel step railings, a handsome and necessary addition to the Church furnishings, were presented by Mrs. Charles Wernlein in memory of her husband. The steps were installed in such a way as to secure the rood screen.

In April, 1983, All Saints Church hosted a gala for their beloved former organist and former choir director, Jean and Robley Lawson. The concert, which was given at the church, included about one hundred singers. Robley conducted a varied program that covered a range of selections from requiems to operas. After the concert, at a dinner in Huske Hall attended by more than two hundred people, the Lawsons were presented with a large purse. Entertainment was provided by a barbershop quartet and other novelty numbers, some of them filled with nostalgia for the two guests of honor. A volunteer band played for dancing after dinner. It was a grand tribute to the Lawsons and "all in all, it seems to me," a vestrymember commented, "that we sponsored an out-

Robley Lawson conducts a concert in Huske Hall

pouring of genuine affection and heartfelt music that reflected most favorably on the Episcopal Church and especially on us.

Venture in Mission (VIM) was a National Episcopal Movement set up about three years earlier to raise one hundred and fifty million dollars to bring the Gospel near and far. Each parish was asked to participate and All Saints was assessed forty-two thousand dollars over a three year period. Father Maier spoke at length with the Bishop about VIM conveying to him that All Saints vestry and parish felt that it had its mission right in Great Neck. In line with this, Father Maier told the Vestry that it would be important to have an Assistant with skills in the areas that were now at a low ebb in the parish. He then recommended Noreen Mooney, who was studying for the Episcopal priesthood and expected to be ordained a Deacon after graduation in June, for the job. She would work part time on specific goals such as the revival of the Sunday School and of *The Herald*, the parish news publication. The Vestry accepted the Rector's proposal and appointed Noreen Mooney Assistant.

Among the new activities by the new Assistant were a Bible study group and an inquirer's class to discuss the Christian faith and the Episcopalian identity.

At the Annual Meeting and cover dish luncheon, J. Charles Frank, Jr. was elected to another term of office as Warden along with three

Vestrymembers. A special tribute was accorded Louis Manzino who was leaving the Vestry but not the work of the Church. Already the recipient of the Parish Service Cross, he was given a gold Episcopal Church emblem. Emblems were presented also to Brock Lownes, who works as a full time volunteer handling the Church's bookkeeping and accounts and to Ladd Jeffers for his prodigious work on the Lawson gala. Laverne Goldberg and Georgette Petchell received gold emblems for their church work.

On Saturday, December 10, 1983, Noreen O'Connor Mooney was ordained to the diaconate at All Saints Church. The Rt. Rev. Robert Campbell Witcher was the celebrant at the beautiful and inspiring service. Other All Saints participants were Father Maier, who preached the sermon, Gerald Houck, Master of Ceremonies, Henry Harvey, the Old Testament reader and Marie Hecht, one of the lay presenters. After the service, a reception was held in the parish house for all the guests. The new Deacon was presented with a check for more than a thousand dollars. Noreen Mooney said of her ordination that it was both an end and a beginning. She spoke of the searching examination of the candidate's whole life and personality and her own wish to know what God is like. And she looked to the celebration of the Sacraments which is both joyful and solemn.

All Saints Nursery School underwent a thorough review to determine its fitness for New York State certification as a licensed Day Care Center. It was approved by the examiners to operate for a full day with a capacity of thirty children. Known as the Great Neck Licensed Day Care Center at All Saints, it became the first such facility on the peninsula.

At the lovely, traditional Christmas Eve Candlelight Service, Captain Kenneth R. Force of the United States Merchant Marine Academy presented All Saints with a banner dedicated to Father Maier. The white silk banner, a magnificent piece of needlework executed in England, is in the shape of a shield. It has a quartered shield within it topped by a faithful copy of the church's rood screen cross. The inner shield has four embroideries of many colored threads depicting favorite symbols in the church which had been chosen by the Vestry. They are: the sacrificial lamb from the stained glass window over the Altar; the facade of the Church, the church seal and an angel with a musical instrument from one of the Tiffany windows. Father Maier and the congregaton were enchanted with the thoughtful and magnificent gift.

The dedication of the parish women to such activities as the Thrift Shop, the bookstore, refunding, the E.C.W. Geranium Card Party, and the two major annual fundraisers, the Christmas Bazaar and the

Strawberry Festival has been so consistent that it has almost been taken for granted. There was a reminder, however, when Mary Schaeffer, aged ninety, retired from management of the Thrift Shop after thirty-one years of service. Another reminder was Dorothy Kelley's report that the St. Catherine's Guild refunding project had brought in five hundred dollars in the past year.

A thank you and farewell party for Noreen Mooney was given on Sunday, June 30th after the 10 A.M. service. She planned to remain at All Saints through July and then "be off to new adventures in the church," Father Maier said. "Her time with us has been most creative," he added. She revived *The Herald*, helped to reestablish the Sunday School and aided in pastoral work. "Noreen's counseling, teaching and communication skills have brought new life to our parish family." The congregation presented Deacon Mooney with a set of vestments.

The retirement of Carol Smith, secretary to the parish since 1965, was another major change that occurred at this time. It was with regret but with wholehearted good wishes that a retirement luncheon was given for her along with gifts and a purse.

All Saints became one of the churches in the forefront of the debate over the ordination of women in the diocese because of its relationship to Barbara Kelley and Noreen Mooney. A statement asking for Rev. Mooney's ordination to the ministry and attesting to her worthiness was made and signed by the entire vestry. The certificate, which recorded her activities in behalf of the parish and stated her value to the parish, was presented to the Diocesan Standing Committee for their action. Up to that time, said Committee had failed to act. Understanding fully that only the Bishop has the right to ordain, the Vestry hoped by its action, to clear any prior obstacles to the ordination.

The 1984 Patronal Festival Service was enhanced by the presence of the Fanfare Trumpeters from the U.S. Merchant Marine Academy. And the occasion was, as always, a time for the remembrance of past parishioners, family and friends.

At the Annual Parish meeting, George Bullen was reelected Warden unanimously along with three Vestrymembers.

The new Vestry started fundraising for the Centennial celebration with an interesting scheme. One hundred tickets would be sold at one hundred dollars a ticket thereby raising ten thousand dollars. At a drawing to be held at the 100th Anniversary dinner dance, the owner of the winning ticket would be presented with a prize of three thousand dollars. Vestry members were asked to undertake the sale of the tickets.

On September 29th, the parish was saddened by the death of Warden

J. Charles Frank, Jr. The Vestry offered a resolution in his memory saying that J. Charles "Buck" Frank served All Saints Church with dedication and love as Vestryman, Warden and Treasurer for many years until his death and . . . was a good and faithful steward as told to us by our Lord Jesus Christ and . . . was beloved by his family, his parish and the community and regarded as a fine Christian gentleman."

Some new fundraising ideas were tried in the Fall of '85. In September, a Garage Sale was set up on the south driveway from Middle Neck Road to the cemetery entrance. Parishioners and others offerd their wares and the Thrift Shop filled the courtyard with fine furniture for sale. The Christmas Bazaar experimented with renting table space to vendors and young people offered child care so that parents were able to shop.

On November 24th, All Saints hosted a luncheon for Dorothy McKechnie, the wife of their former Rector, in honor of her ninetieth birthday. In addition to her family and the parishioners, representatives of the Great Neck Women's Club and the D.A.R., two organizations in which Mrs. McKechnie had been very active, were present.

The Annual Parish Meeting of 1985 was a memorable one for many reasons. It was the start of the centennial year. It was also the twentieth anniversary of Father Maier's ministry at All Saints. The ECW presented him with a book that had been compiled in his honor containing "thoughts and memories from all the people who love you." He was presented also with a purse of five thousand dollars and a new ceremonial cope from the parishioners.

Warden-elect Ladd Jeffers talked about the proposed budget for the 100th year. It endeavored to open new avenues of resources, he said, and to pass on stewardship to every parishioner. While he admitted that he was optimistic, had even, perhaps, indulged in wishful thinking in his projections, he added some sound truths as warnings. Our endowment is a cushion but will not keep us long, he cautioned. It is not a catchall to bail us out anymore. We no longer have a grand patron. Each of us must contribute with imagination and hard work so that we can pay our own way. During the 100th, we must try to rebuild our endowment.

In that spirit, the Young People's Fellowship started its sale of 100th Anniversary bumper stickers. The Altar Guild sponsored a giant Christmas card upon which donors' names were inscribed.

The meeting concluded with the unanimous election of Ladd Jeffers as Warden and three Vestrymembers.

The anniversary year opened with more plans for the celebration. A pictorial directory of all parish members was projected to be ready no later than October, 1986. Commemorative plates, mugs, coasters and notecards were ordered and would be available to go on sale at the Strawberry Festival.

Other parish matters were given serious consideration by the Vestry. Once again the size of the vestry was argued. Some felt it was too large and cumbersome for a parish the size of All Saints and, further, that some vestrymembers attended infrequently. Others pointed out, again, that a larger vestry encouraged more people to be involved with the church. A motion was made to reduce the numbers on the Vestry by attrition but it failed to be adopted.

Five hundred copies of the revised churchyard rules were printed. The expectation was that these new rules would stop some of the current abuses by cemetery plot owners such as excessive plantings that extended too far and the display of artificial flowers on the plots.

Some of the parishioners had expressed concern over the quality of the music program which, in their view, was deteriorating. To remedy this, since Brink Bush, the organist, did not want to direct the choir, Jim Sergi was made the choir director.

The Strawberry Festival for the 100th was planned as a two day project, Saturday as well as Friday, an ambitious undertaking but one that proved to be very successful as was the centennial journal. Together the festival and journal brought in about sixteen thousand dollars.

Two very welcome gifts were donated at this time. The Rudolph Kopf estate gave a sizable sum of money and Jim and Kass Rogers presented a young copper beech tree to replace the venerable old one that had to be cut down because of disease. Therefore, as All Saints entered its second century, it could be known again as "the belfry and the beech." The Gignoux plot, another church landmark, was restored and the stone replaced.

As the day of the 100th Anniversary Service approached, carefully laid out plans were carried out. Warden Jeffers assembled a choir of about sixty voices. Jean and Robley Lawson planned to come up from Florida to play the organ and to conduct the choir and Westchester Brass Quintet. Captain Kenneth Force arranged for the Fanfare Trumpeters from the U.S. Merchant Marine Academy and also agreed to compose a special musical tribute for the occasion.

In October, Bishop Witcher, who was to be the celebrant on the great day, sent an an inspiring letter to Father Maier and the members of All Saints Church. He wrote that "Your place in Great Neck is significant for the local community as well as for the Diocese. Your churchyard serves as a symbol of community not only of All Saints Church, but also the Diocese of Long Island, since it is the burial place of our first Bishop. But

The Rt. Rev. Robert C. Witcher, Bishop of Long Island, celebrant at the 100th anniversary

the past should only remind us of our present status and the future ministry offered to all people in Great Neck. I know that you will use this occasion not only to celebrate the past, but to plan the future as well."

On Saturday, November 1, 1986, All Saints Church marked its 100th Anniversary with a joyous celebration. While the procession, composed of the 100th Anniversary Choir, the All Saints Wardens and Vestry, the visiting clergy from other Churches and Synagogues, leaders of the com-

All Saints Church 100th Anniversary Service. *Hon. Sol Wachtler* reading the 23rd Psalm.

munity and Prelates formed outside of the Church, the proceedings began inside the packed Church with the glorious strains of "The Trumpet Shall Sound" from Handel's "Messiah;" Joseph Greco and Peter Maravell soloists. The Fanfare Trumpets pealed. Then the procession entered singing Vaughn Williams' "For All The Saints."

All Saints Church 100th Anniversary Service view of Altar, choir and musicians.

There were several faiths represented at the service: the Rev. Joseph E. Dunn, Rector of St. Aloysius R.C. Church, Great Neck, the Rev. Gary Hasse, Pastor of the Community Church, Great Neck and Rabbi Robert Widom of Temple Emanuel, Great Neck. The Rev. John Mulryan of St. Paul's Episcopal Church, Great Neck was also present. Among the public figures who attended were Town Supervisor John B. Kiernan and State Senator Frank Padavan. The Hon. Sol Wachtler, Chief Justice of the New

York State Board of Appeals, read the 23rd Psalm, and Rabbi Widom read the Old Testament lesson, 1 Kings 8: 2-30. The Epistle was read by Henry Harvey, Warden Emeritus of All Saints Church and the Gospel, Matthew 3: 1-12, by the Very Rev. Robert Wilshire, Dean of Long Island.

All Saints Church was honored to have as Celebrant for this historic service, the Rt. Rev. Robert Campbell Witcher, Bishop of Long Island. Father Gary E. Maier, Rector of All Saints, delivered the sermon which was based on the text, "Rejoice, be exceeding glad for great is your reward in heaven." Father Maier asked those assembled to join him in looking back one hundred years and "see how the founders of this Church followed the commission of the Beatitudes and have shown forth their light in this community to bring All Saints Church into reality." He reminded the listeners that in 1886, Great Neck was a wealthy community of estates, farms and a small village at the northern end of the peninsula. There was no church.

Proudly, Father Maier spoke of the missionary outreach of the parish—the building of its daughter church, St. Paul's. He described the missionary zeal of this parish which, during his years as Rector, "created our own diaspora throughout the Episcopal Church, not only in this country but throughout the world." Many of those who had served as curates and assistants were present this night. Some of them had grown up in the parish.

Perhaps the most moving parts of the sermon, because they spoke to all those present, were the passages on ecumenicalism and community service.

The Church is the people, the body of Christ. Over the years there has been a wonderful relationship between this church and the community. "Working together, Jews, Catholics and Protestants have accomplished many good works such as the North Shore University Hospital, the Scouts, Alcoholics Anonymous and numerous youth groups. So this is an evening when we should all be proud. Although we come from different faiths, we are one in our belief in God ... and we are one in our common humanity and struggles to make our community a better place to live ... We are all to be peacemakers under God's love and guidance."

After the sermon, Father Maier presented Jerusalem crosses to Dorothy McKechnie, Dorothy Burke and Bobbi Grose for their outstanding contributions to the parish.

Music of soaring and gladsome beauty pervaded the service. John Alexander, a leading tenor of the Metropolitan Opera company, sang during the communion service. An original piece, appropriately called "Jubilance," composed by Captain Kenneth R. Force especially for the 100th, expressed eloquently the joy of the occasion.

Presentation of the Proclamation declaring November 1st All Saints Day in the town of North Hempstead. (Reading L to R) Sen. Frank Padavan, John Kiernan, Supervisor of the Town of North Hempstead, Fr. Maier, Hon. John Da Vanzo, Judge Jules Orenstein, County Court

At the reception following the Church service, John B. Kiernan, Supervisor of the Town of North Hempstead, reiterated All Saints' dedicated one hundred years of service to the Great Neck community. He presented Father Maier with a Proclamation declaring November 1st All Saints Day in the town of North Hempstead. Mr. Kiernan said that although All Saints Day has long been on the liturgical calendar, he wanted to add it to the Town of North Hempstead calendar.

A gala dinner, attended by more than two hundred people, concluded the evening's activities. Huske Hall, decorated with flowers and hung with balloons, was the scene of dancing to the music of Jim Rogers' "Long Island Sounds." Florence Bromley won the drawing for the three thousand dollar centennial prize. At midnight, the guests disbursed aware that such a celebration could not be repeated for a century.

An important event that occurred before the end of the centennial year was the ordination of Gerald Houck, All Saints' Administrator, to the Diaconate. The awesome service took place at the Cathedral of the Incarnation, Garden City and was celebrated by Bishop Witcher. Many All Saints parishioners attended the ceremony and their ordinand was presented by Father and Mrs. Maier, Bobbi Grose, Mimi Frank and Patricia and Joseph Lediger.

The parish gave a reception for the new Deacon, now the Curate of All Saints, after the December 21st Sunday Service of Lessons and Carols. The Rev. Houck was presented with a silver communion set from the E.C.W. and a check from the congregation.

Deacon Houck reciprocated by placing Father Maier and All Saints Church among the stars. Officially recorded, the Rev. Gary E. Maier star is Orion R A 6h 12mOsd 9o 46". The All Saints Church star is Ursa Major R A 10h54m 14sd 40o 59."

The last Annual Parish Meeting of the Church's first hundred years was very well attended. The atmosphere was one of positive feelings about the present, hope for the future and respect and gratitude towards those who had carried the church thus far through good times and bad.

The polls were opened by Father Maier who introduced the candidates presented by the Nominating Committee. Marie B. Hecht was the first woman to be proposed for Warden of All Saints Church, perhaps the first in the Diocese. Brock Lownes, Almoner and former Vestryman and James Rogers, Chairman of the Cemetery Committee and former Vestryman were proposed for the new Vestry as were Gerald Egan, Kenneth Force, Laurie MacLean and Barbara C. Neale. There were no nominations from the floor.

Marie Hecht gave a talk called "Some thoughts on All Saints Church's One Hundred Years of History," all of which appears in expanded form in these pages. She concluded with — "While I was working on the history, one line, a paraphrase of Daniel Webster's famous words, kept running through my mind –"She's a small Church, but those who know her love her."

The Every Member Canvass, chaired by John C. Cavanaugh, using a Pony Express theme to personalize the collection of the pledges, increased the number of pledges considerably. In general, Warden Ladd Jeffers said, stewardship was up because our parish wants more as, for example, an expanded music program. "We're making considerable progress financially," he added, "and next year we want to do better."

Myriad change has occurred in the world, in the nation and in Great Neck since a small band of dedicated men met to plan the founding of All Saints Church. From a community of farms and estates, Great Neck has grown into a well populated peninsula that is threatening to become a small city. A predominantly Christian, heavily Episcopalian population is now predominantly Jewish and Roman Catholic. All Saints' congregation, one hundred years ago, was almost entirely white, wealthy and of Anglo Saxon origin. Now, people of all races and many ethnic origins compose the All Saints family.

The Church has endured because it continues to show signs of new life, new outreach and new dedication. The will to provide spiritual growth and community service is, perhaps, stronger now than it was one hundred years ago because it is more needed. With God's help, All Saints Church will meet the challenge of the next millenium and provide spiritual care for the generations to come during its second hundred years.